CURRICULUM DESIGN
A HANDBOOK FOR EDUCATORS

CURRICULUM DESIGN
A HANDBOOK FOR EDUCATORS

Kathleen M. Wulf
UNIVERSITY OF SOUTHERN CALIFORNIA

Barbara Schave
UNIVERSITY OF SOUTHERN CALIFORNIA

Scott, Foresman and Company
GLENVIEW, ILLINOIS   LONDON

To our husbands, Bob and Doug

48, From "A Model for Curriculum Design Using a Systems Approach" by T. E. Cyrs, Jr. and R. Lowenthal in AUDIOVISUAL INSTRUCTION, Vol. 15, January 1970, pp. 16–18. Copyright © 1970 by the Association for Educational Communications and Technology. Reprinted by permission; **90,** From MAKING THE CLASSROOM TEST: A GUIDE FOR TEACHERS, Third Edition. Copyright © 1973 by Educational Testing Service. Reprinted by permission; **94–95,** From MEASURING EDUCATIONAL OUTCOMES: FUNDAMENTALS OF TESTING by Bruce W. Tuckman. Copyright © 1975 by Harcourt Brace Jovanovich, Inc., and reprinted with their permission; **108,** From HANDBOOK IN RESEARCH AND EVALUATION by Stephen Isaac in collaboration with William B. Michael. Copyright © 1977 by EdITS Publishers, San Diego, CA 92107. Reprinted by permission; **112–13,** "Prototypes of Curriculum Evaluation" by Robert E. Stake, CIRCE, University of Illinois, October 1969. Reprinted by permission; **150–53,** From "Instrumentation of Bloom's and Krathwohl's Taxonomies for the Writing of Educational Objectives" by N. S. Metfessel, W. B. Michael, and D. S. Kirsner, in PSYCHOLOGY IN THE SCHOOLS, Vol. II, No. 3, July 1969, pp. 227–231. Reprinted by permission; **154,** From A TAXONOMY OF THE PSYCHOMOTOR DOMAIN: *A Guide for Developing Behavioral Objectives* by Anita J. Harrow. Copyright © 1972 by Longman Inc. Reprinted with permission of Longman Inc., New York; **163–67,** From DEVELOPING AN INSTRUMENT FOR ASSESSMENT OF INSTRUCTIONAL MATERIALS (Form IV) by Maurice J. Eash. American Educational Research Association Annual Convention, Minneapolis, March 1970. Reprinted by permission of the author.

Library of Congress Cataloging in Publication Data

Wulf, Kathleen,
    Curriculum design.
    Includes bibliographies and index.
    1. Curriculum planning—United States. 2. Teaching teams—United States. 3. Curriculum planning—California —Los Angeles Metropolitan Area—Case studies. I. Schave, Barbara. II. Title.
LB1570.W85 1984   375'.001   84-1294

    4 5 6-MAL-89 88 87 86

FOREWORD

There is at present great national interest in strengthening the curriculum in the direction of academic excellence—particularly in the areas of math, science, and computer literacy. At the same time there is something else in the wind—a growing concern for general education. All across the country, school staffs are interested in revising their curricula so that all students explore shared values, reaffirm goals, and confront common problems. If this were not enough, more than thirty national projects have addressed concerns about outdated content, low standards, differentiated treatment of the sexes and minority students, and failure to equip students with the tools they need for employment.

Clearly the national mood points to the need for persons knowledgeable in procedures for designing lessons and materials appropriate for new ideas and aims. Indeed, a serious challenge is how to design instruction that will enable members of underprivileged underclasses to have success with quality content formerly available only to a small elite.

Curriculum development at the local level is on center stage. This is so, in part, because we now recognize that curriculum must be adapted to local interests and to the particular individuals to be served. There is a dilemma of how best to balance the demand for programs in response to national needs with the requirements of local communities. A further reason for the popularity of local curriculum development rests on the desire for effective schools. Effective schools have a strong sense of community, commonly shared goals, and high expectations for students and staff performance. Successful schools are characterized by staff interactions involving aspects of teaching whereby administrators and teachers work together in planning, designing, evaluating, and preparing materials for teaching. It is through the designing of curriculum and collective decision-making that teacher efficacy is enhanced.

How then can teachers, administrators, community groups, and individuals best develop the materials, courses, and programs to meet new demands? *Curriculum Design* aims at answering this question. The book is a practical guide for instructional planning in order to achieve new goals. Essential phases of the design process are treated, including selecting content, converting goals to instructional objectives, generating and organizing appropriate learning opportunities, and verifying the worth of the programs developed. An unusual feature of the book is the attention given to organizing for a team approach to the design project. Readers are helped to relate what they already know to the tasks of curriculum making. Curriculum specialists and novices alike will find the procedural steps for designing curriculum sensible and effective. These procedures are presented with the specificity of detail desired by practitioners.

The authors, Kathleen Wulf and Barbara Schave, are experienced in designing curriculum, having developed numerous courses and materials in a range of situations and in different content fields. The useful exercises and illustrations in the text are based upon the successful curriculum design activities of the authors.

The authors do not try to include everything about curriculum. They don't focus on large political, economic, and administrative commitments or engage in philosophical theorizing about the ends of education. Instead, they emphasize procedural treatments that are necessary for the achievement of desired goals. Nevertheless, members of curriculum project teams in schools and students in formal classrooms studying the curriculum-making process, will find that *Curriculum Design* stimulates the kind of deliberation—the coalescence of aims, data, and judgments—that makes creative curriculum planning possible.

John D. McNeil
UCLA

PREFACE

Curriculum development has been the concern of educators since the beginning of "formal" education in Grecian times. In general, theories on how to design curriculum range from a very rigid approach, exemplified by the subject-centered curriculum which addresses learning in terms of the body of knowledge to be digested and internalized, to a very open-ended approach, exemplified by the humanists who view learning as a process of self-realization and self-actualization. In the middle of this continuum are the social reconstructionists who view learning as a problem-solving, pragmatic process for understanding the issues facing humanity. More radical theories of curriculum define what happens in school as an art, as a science, or as an existential process.

Traditional theories of curriculum are integrated into schooling at different levels of learning. Radical theories of curriculum are more pertinent to the academic community and experimental schools. It becomes apparent in exploring curriculum that the issue is not that we do not have enough theories or the correct theories. The problem is that we do not know how to apply these theories to schooling.

Anybody who has ever attempted to "teach" would agree that the gap between theory and practice in education is wide and deep. Further, those teachers who try to bridge this gap are few and far between. Speculatively, this can be attributed to two factors. First, there is a general disregard by practitioners for theories of curriculum design and implementation, which belong to the professors who supposedly never leave their "ivory towers" to see what it is like in "the real world" of teaching. Secondly, teachers are so used to working from established curricula whether in reading, math, science, or physical education that they "panic" at the thought of designing new curricular concepts themselves. They don't know how to do it because they have never been taught.

The issue is further complicated by strategies for change imposed upon schools, administrators, teachers, and students by federal or state governments, the universities, or other agencies who want to "help out." In actuality, these agencies frequently serve to alienate and confuse teachers who could probably implement change if they had a way to approach the problem of designing new curriculum in order to achieve new goals.

We contend that change and growth are internal to the individual, and thus to institutions; change and growth cannot be imposed from the outside. The purpose of this book, then, is to present a systematic approach for those teachers and administrators who want to bring new concepts to their students through curriculum design. This book shows educators how to bring about change in curriculum.

Our approach is based on our combined twenty-five years of experience in designing and implementing curriculum. This approach has been used at all levels of education from early childhood through high school, college, and graduate and professional education — and not only in the United States but also in Europe and the Far East. It works!

Our entire book rests on one fundamental assumption: teachers *can* develop curriculum. It is our conviction that not only can teachers and graduate students develop a curriculum, but with training in this book's sequential method, they can do it as well as or even better than "outsiders" can.

A word about our own intellectual sympathies. The theory and method that inform our work are rooted in: Bruner's spiral curriculum, the concept that you can teach any subject at any level; Piaget's concept of learning as an active process that is meaningful to the learner; Ausubel's research on meaningful receptive learning and "advance organizers"; and Gagne's and Mager's hierarchical strategy approach to instruction.

Finally, *A Solar Energy Curriculum for Elementary Schools* is employed here as an example of our approach integrating curriculum theory with hands-on experience in curriculum design and implementation. Under a grant from the U.S. Department of Energy and with teachers from the Los Angeles metropolitan area, this solar energy curriculum was designed and put into practice according to our model. It is used throughout this book to illustrate the phases and sequence of our curriculum design. This project was chosen as an example because it addressed a subject area in which no sequential curriculum existed, in which comprehensive materials were not available, and in which the teacher members were not previously experienced at designing curriculum.

ACKNOWLEDGMENTS

We would like to thank Elliot Eisner, John D. McNeil, Ian Westbury, Kenneth T. Henson, and Robert Zais for their helpful comments.

KMW
BS

CONTENTS

CHAPTER 1

UNDERSTANDING THE ELEMENTS OF CURRICULUM DESIGN

If you don't know where you're going, then any path will take you there.

The Cheshire Cat

Changes in society brought about by changes in the traditional family structure, in addition to the knowledge explosion centered on teaching, learning and development, have had a major impact on education today (Saylor, Alexander, & Lewis 1981). The reality that teachers must meet more of the total needs of their students, with psychological insight based on knowledge gained from learning and development theory as well as from instructional technology, is apparent to anyone concerned with meaningful educational experiences.

How will the teacher function in this new way? Budget cuts are so severe that consultants are considered a luxury to be used for deficiencies in the school, but not for innovation. Federal and state support for schools sometimes present more problems than they solve. For example, the federal law requiring an Individualized Educational Program for each special needs child in the least restrictive environment (PL 94–142) requires specific curriculum design of each school district within the United States, but gives educators little help in explaining how the new curriculum should be designed or how such a massive undertaking can be adequately funded. Such legislation, while aiming at the common good, provides guidelines and requirements, but little help beyond that point, thus leaving the local professional staff to cope with the demands placed upon their time and resources.

The large body of research devoted to curriculum innovation is based on theories that are themselves hard to implement. Further, as McNeil (1981) points out, academic strategies for change are very often unrealistically focused on the success of the project, not the success of the school and students.

Educators—that is, teachers and administrators—are now faced with the challenge of proceeding with the necessary changes themselves or sticking with curriculum and instruction that has not successfully met the needs of the learners. On initially facing this challenge, the educator might feel strongly that the Cheshire Cat is wise—"If you don't know where you are going, then any path will take you there." Reflecting upon this issue, however, leads the educator to seek out an approach for designing new curriculum that will meet the needs of the learner.

THE APPROACH OF THIS BOOK

This book presents a plan for designing curriculum that can be used by the undergraduate or the graduate in a curriculum course, or by a school staff without the continued use of outside money or expertise. The model presented in this book is based on a systems approach which has been used extensively in industry, finance, engineering, and management. A systems approach is a planning tool, organized to deal with a group of observable variables that affect one another. In education it is an experience-based model, a process to identify the elements, relationships, and sequences of a learning experience for a team of teachers, or an individual, to produce curriculum materials (Romiszowski 1982).

The initial premise of this approach is that group interaction and group goals are the most effective means for designing meaningful curriculum. Practicality, sequence, and logic are a part of the group process, which is divided into three distinct phases:

1. Problem Definition
2. Development
3. Evaluation

Together these phases include the elements of curriculum design:

1. Identifying a purpose
2. Selecting designer participants
3. Selecting the content of curriculum
4. Writing goals for learners
5. Learning about instructional objectives

6. Turning goals into instructional objectives
7. Generating appropriate lessons
8. Developing instructional materials
9. Recommending a learning environment
10. Evaluating outcomes
11. Continuing feedback

These are all essential to the development of any curriculum and should be sequenced in the manner suggested to attain a coherent learning outcome.

In the problem-definition phase, the critical point is that a connection be made between the content, as defined, and the group of participants who have been selected. The project must reflect the "needs" of the participants. If this purpose is not entirely clear, a needs assessment, which is a public process that elicits the opinions of parents, teachers, students, politicians, academicians, sociologists, and community agencies, should be considered (Pratt 1980).

The second phase, development, includes six elements of curriculum design. First, the selection of the content must be delineated through research, theory, expert help, or needs assessment. From this content, goals for learners are developed which reflect the theory and philosophy of the identified content. Instructional objectives are derived from the goals, and lessons are then generated. The next task of this development phase is to organize appropriate materials for use with the established lesson plans and to recommend a learning environment for the implementation of the newly designed curriculum.

The final phase contains two critical elements: evaluation and feedback. Evaluation can be carried out in different ways depending on the nature of the learning activities. Feedback is continued throughout the process but is particularly relevant in the evaluation phase where new materials and strategies may be necessary to correct problems that have arisen (See Figure 1.1).

RESISTANCE TO THIS APPROACH

An organized model of curriculum design has become the norm in military and industrial education, but it has not had a marked impact upon public or private education. There have been some fundamental reasons for avoiding this type of approach.

First, educators have assumed that a group approach to curriculum design would not be cost-effective. They have been awed by the "think tank" method of developing materials with large resident staffs, "unlimited" time to devote to the task, and the large sample response necessary for impressive evaluation reports. Educators have considered this approach grandiose, expensive, and unwieldy in small, local-scale situations.

Another substantial reason for reluctance to implement a group

FIGURE 1.1
A Model for Curriculum Design

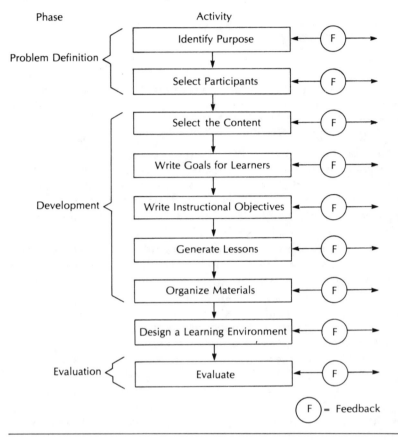

approach has been a lack of teacher participation in designing curriculum. Traditionally, a faculty curriculum committee for a particular school district does not generate lessons; rather, they review materials already produced elsewhere. They have practice in being consumers but no practice as designers. Even in optimal professional training, very few undergraduates or graduate students have been taught how to make a curricular module of their own.

Another critical reason for not employing this type of approach has been the reluctance of many educators to adopt any strict instructional strategy for teaching and learning. Arguing that stating objectives in specific behavioral terms limits humanistic outcomes (i.e., spontaneity), some educators fear a step-by-step approach in education may stifle creativity. Others fear that criterion-referenced testing will demonstrate that learners have not mastered the content sufficiently, and then teachers might be held accountable for their students' failures.

WHAT THIS APPROACH CAN ACCOMPLISH FOR GROUPS AND INDIVIDUALS

The approach suggested in this book has several distinct advantages. It can be cost-effective. Students can use it in curriculum courses. Teachers can do it with even more insight than "outside experts." The process need not be rigid and behavioristic. It is aimed at a variety of curricular tasks, regardless of the age of the learners or the nature of the content.

This approach is a group process—an enabling process which constitutes a framework for each individual effort at curriculum design. Here are some examples of the problems that can be solved with this method:

Development of a first-generation course design. At present there is an ongoing demand for schools and universities to create and mount "instant" courses or curricular units in areas which previously have not been a part of curriculum. Such demands require that work must be produced quickly and instantaneously adopted.

Curriculum integration. Throughout the field of education, there is a growing push to integrate existing areas of curriculum into inter-disciplinary approaches. As faculties interact to synthesize existing courses, a systematic process helps to create the new structures.

Departmental redesign. In most educational institutions, faculties and advisory committees periodically redesign their course content and offerings. This approach helps such a group address the problem.

Creation of new programs. This task combines any two of the above. The innovative process in institutional settings means that most schools are constantly creating new pilot settings. The necessary steps of problem definition, development, and evaluation again may be applied.

Creation of curriculum for new schools. Every new school has a new philosophy and a special population to serve. They need new curriculum materials, which this approach will provide.

Class Project in Graduate Course in Curriculum. This book may be used by individual students or by groups of students who make up the development team.

In summary, this approach provides a comprehensive, integrated, and practical plan to achieve specific goals in an educational setting for either an individual or a group.

THE FRAMEWORK OF THIS APPROACH

In an effort to realistically adapt this approach to curricular tasks in various settings, five critical assumptions are made. These assumptions are applicable to an individual who is learning how to use this approach.

1. *Group Interaction.* Each of the curricular efforts operates within a small group, which consists of five to thirty-five participant-practitioners.
2. *Implementation.* Members of the development team will be the first implementers of the produced lessons.
3. *Costs.* Time and funding for development of the new program are minimal.
4. *Personnel.* Prior to participation, the individual practitioners are not specialists in course design. They possess instructional, not necessarily managerial, skills.
5. *Level of participation.* The need for participant involvement in evaluation and revision tasks will be ongoing.

From the established framework, this approach has been designed to meet some basic assumptions about curriculum:

1. *Practical.* The process must be practical in view of the limited time available. A curriculum design plan that is overburdened with flow charts and needless steps is a time waster. Conversely, however, an open-structured "no-plan" is a disaster as well.
2. *Begins at beginning.* The process must train participants in necessary skills as they work through the appropriate steps. Requisite skills must not be assumed.
3. *Designed for participants.* Each of the strategies of curriculum design learned in the process must have functional application in that participant's own instructional setting.
4. *Replication.* The participants, as a team with their own established skills and abilities, must be able to replicate the process with other curricular tasks, without the need for an outside consultant.

The ultimate goal for teachers or students who participate in this method of curriculum design is that they transfer their expertise as members of new curriculum design teams—or, perhaps in an even more important role, that they lead new groups in a "trainer of trainers" strategy. Each participant will experience the various steps in this approach personally, entering into the tasks required, not simply observing the behavior of others. In that respect, participation in this approach to new design of curriculum is a form of inservice training for teachers, a form of professional growth for other educators.

Each of the steps in the developmental process is precisely defined for all participants. Appropriate forms to stimulate responses are included. Necessary behavioral skills are stated for each step in the process. Finally, evaluation and feedback methods for group and self-appraisal are built in.

HOW THIS BOOK IS ORGANIZED

This chapter has described the elements of curriculum design. The remainder of the book is organized to achieve mastery of each necessary skill in this approach.

Chapter 2 addresses the task of participating as a team member and sets the stage for each participant's expectations and responsibilities for the curriculum design project. We emphasize that in this method, unlike some "committee work," all members are participants and there are no bystanders. Some guidelines for managing are given, complete with plans for structuring sessions for work, reports, and feedback. A system of accountability to the group evolves. The chapter reviews some principles of group dynamics and suggests strategies for building a commitment to teamwork with a sense of mutual trust. Suggestions for individual use of this approach are included.

Chapter 3 deals with selecting the content of curriculum. Assuming the team or an individual has established a philosophy from which to work, or that a philosophy has been established for them already by the governing body of their institution, they are ready to ask, "Why are we designing a new curriculum?" "What problems are we addressing?" "What does our mandate require us to emphasize in our curricular project?"

Whether it is an attempt at redefinition of a course or a beginning of a new design altogether, the group or the individual must begin by describing what is presently taught. This includes analyzing text and curricular guidelines as they presently exist. Then the existing model is evaluated. In the event that nothing exists in the target area, an initial research process must take place with available subject matter experts or with written resources, or a needs assessment must be implemented.

From this point the participants select the content. The existing curriculum can serve as a rudimentary basis for the new structure, or perhaps a new selection of content will emerge from subject matter, expert input, group research, or needs assessment. More specifically, the critical parts of the content area are identified, providing a core organizer for the subject experts in the role of "teacher" to the rest of the group. A flow chart of central concepts can be established as the final model, with each section coded with a corresponding letter or number. Later this structure of the content model serves as an organizational outline for the subsequent steps in the design process.

Chapter 4 describes the writing of goals for learners. Goals that are established are based upon the thinking of the team or the individual when they delineate the end result for this project. Goal writing, of all steps in this course design process, is most familiar to participants, and probably will not be a new skill for them. Nevertheless, some theoretical background in goal setting from educational psychology literature is provided. Then participants state goals in general language for the entire curricular project. Checks may be made against the structure of the content model to ascertain that all relevant subject parts are addressed.

Understanding the nature or the relationship between goals and effective instructional objectives is the task outlined in Chapter 5, which also presents an overview of instructional objectives.

Chapter 6 begins by describing various models of objective writing from the work of Bloom, Mager, Michael, and others; a clear process of deriving objectives from goals is advocated. In emphasizing instructional statements of student learning outcomes, this chapter explores the levels of educational objectives in cognitive, affective, and psychomotor domains. Reference material to help in devising individual objective statements is included. Various parts of an objective—that is, the audience, the behavior, the conditions of learning, and the degree of mastery—are delineated. Appropriate forms are recommended and examples are cited.

Chapter 7 describes how, objective by objective, the project team tackles the task of writing lessons. Each team member uses an agreed-upon format or the form included. Whatever their form, however, these lessons show one distinct advantage over much present-day curriculum development. They emerge from a central agreed-upon point of departure. Each lesson can be traced back through its objective to a general goal based on the agreed-upon curriculum. Therefore, no lesson stands alone because it is novel or cute or fun; rather, each lesson is part of an instructional system.

Chapter 8 discusses how to select and prepare resource materials for teachers and students. Questions of "What do we need?" are answered by analyzing the lessons produced during the Chapter 7 phase. When a film strip, a student workbook, or a demonstration device is required, the name of the material is placed on a master list for materials development. That list then serves as a "shopping guide" for resources to be found or resources to be generated. In some cases, a special instructor's package of information may be the critical material needed.

Chapter 9 describes how to design a learning environment with attention to the physical, social, and psychological aspects of learning.

Finally, an evaluation plan is prepared. In Chapter 10 the problem of deciding upon evaluation is addressed, stressing that at this point, because of the work already completed, the criterion items may be easily adapted from the instructional objectives. Relying upon a criterion-referenced approach, evaluation is possible through a variety of strategies: teacher observation, student achievement data, student self-report, and many others. Initially, materials for formative evaluation of the curriculum design are produced. These aid in validating the new lessons in pilot test situations. Subsequently, as a result of that feedback, revisions and improvements are made and then summary instruments of evaluation prepared.

The crucial step in this process is, of course, *feedback*. The project team has not completed its task until the feedback is incorporated into its revisions. This may mean returning to an earlier step (e.g., lesson writing) to more effectively achieve the stated goals. If there are gaps in the logical progression of lessons from one concept to the next, it will be apparent in the pilot test. Similarly, if more evaluation instruments are necessary, the lack of data will point to that need. If it appears that learners need more work on antecedent concepts (i.e., entering behaviors) required to begin study in a content area, then changes will be made back in the process of preparing objectives. Since feedback loops exist to all earlier steps, revision is always possible.

To facilitate learning, each chapter contains a summary of the content of that section, questions to think about, appropriate examples of useful forms and real outcomes, and follow-up activities.

Appendix A contains some pieces of curricular development which illustrate our approach applied to a problem of course design. Entitled *A Solar Energy Curriculum for Elementary Schools,* this example is a genuine series of lessons developed by the authors, consulting with a team of teachers and subject matter experts during 1978–82. Appendix B, entitled "The Cognitive, Affective, and Psychomotor Domains," presents reference material on instructional objectives which supports activities during the Chapter 5 objective writing stage. Appendix C contains two model lessons from a critical thinking curriculum, each illustrating a format suitable for use during the generating of lessons (Chapter 7). Appendix D is "An Instrument for the Assessment of Instructional Material," developed by Maurice J. Eash. All materials can be judged according to these criteria during the selection process in Chapter 8.

FOLLOW-UP ACTIVITIES

1. Explain in your own words what the elements of curriculum design are, as defined in this approach.
2. Identify the sequential steps in this group process.
3. Select a curriculum project, real or hypothetical, that your group or that you as an individual can use for applying skills to be acquired in subsequent chapters.
4. State the advantages of orderly development of a curriculum.
5. Give reasons why feedback at the various stages of curriculum development is critical.

REFERENCES

McNeil, J. *Curriculum: A Comprehensive Introduction*. Boston: Little, Brown & Co., 1981.

Pratt, D. *Curriculum Development and Design*. San Francisco: Harcourt Brace Jovanovich, 1980.

Romiszowski, A. J. "A New Look At Instructional Design Part II Instruction: Integrating One's Approach." *British Journal of Educational Technology* 13 (1982): 15–55.

Saylor, J. G.; Alexander, W. A.; & Lewis, A. J. *Curriculum Planning for Better Teaching and Learning* 4th ed. New York: Holt, Rinehart & Winston, 1981.

CHAPTER 2

PARTICIPATING AS A TEAM MEMBER

Work expands to fill the available time.

Parkinson's Law

Assuming that Parkinson was right, and anyone who has ever served on a curriculum committee knows that he was, a major concern of the project team members is to organize themselves for maximum effectiveness. Since time and personnel are limited, particularly in these days of reduced funding for education, each hour must count. This chapter reviews information about the psychology of groups and the effect of group interaction on changing the face of education. The difficulties of how to turn an assemblage of individuals into a group, how to help them accept a new organization, and how to be most productive in their task are then discussed.

For undergraduates, graduates, or individuals implementing this approach, this chapter is important for two additional reasons. First, the professional educator, or aspiring educator, will be able to serve as a group leader after using the model advocated in this book. And second, the leader will be able to teach this model of curriculum design to others. Understanding curriculum theory by itself is not enough; the educator must experience the complexity of curriculum design. Therefore, individuals working alone should read this team approach chapter as well.

PSYCHOLOGY OF GROUPS

All of us in education have known since the famous Lewin, Lippitt, and White (1939) study that authoritarian leadership fosters maximum group output. More recent research and our own experience, however, suggest that democratic leadership is more beneficial to society. We recall that when groups of boys worked under authoritarian leadership, they produced the most work; however, when the leader left, the work stopped. In the democratic group, work continued in spite of the leader's absence. Other studies in factories demonstrated similar results; that is, when there was some reward, some motivation, or some cooperation among participants, morale tended to be higher and production remained at a higher level.

More than thirty years ago, Kurt Lewin (1952) observed that social institutions resemble individuals in that they develop customary ways of behaving to insure an orderly progress toward institutional goals. Members of these institutional groups are expected to conform to these customary behaviors or norms. Rules of dress, punctuality, peer group relationships, and even attitudes of the individual members toward the institution itself reflect this pressure for conformity. Deviant behavior is often rejected, the individual soon realizing that such behavior will not be accepted by the group.

Of course, such norms are desirable in that they make it possible for members of the organization to work together toward some shared goal. How to effect changes in group norms was the subject of Lewin's study on altering the norms of eating. One conclusion from this study was that group commitment and participation in the setting of new norms were more influential in changing behavior than individual attempts to change such norms. It was this demonstration that a group can modify and reinforce its members' commitments to changing norms that led industrial psychologists to explore further the concept of participatory management.

As early as the late 1940s, Koch and French (1948) utilized this principle in an authoritative study on the productivity of girls in a pajama factory. By involving production workers in setting new production quotas, resulting from changes in the design of pajamas, the investigators established a correlation between the level of group participation and a willingness to accept new production quotas without the usual resistance to change.

In the 1980s, there is increasing interest in group management techniques, particularly when economic success is an outcome. The Japanese experience in producing automobiles is bringing about changes in managerial structure and style in the United States. Research on the Japanese factory productivity, personnel morale, and willingness to change suggests that personal involvement in the task pays off.

GROUP INTERACTION EFFECTS CHANGE IN EDUCATION

The literature on change strategies in education suggests the use of group interaction as a valuable tool (Eisner 1979). In fact, Oliva

(1982) indicates that group interaction is the key to curriculum development.

A Rand Study (Berman & McLaughlin 1977) analyzing federal programs supporting change concluded that four characteristics of educational institutions are necessary for change to occur: 1. top-down, bottom-up planning, 2. school principal involvement, 3. teacher efficacy (i.e., teacher thinks he or she can do it!), and 4. on-going staff development. This research is pertinent to curriculum design.

The work of Johnson and Johnson (1975) with elementary and junior high school students suggests that cooperative goal structures positively affect learning. They indicate that group goal structure and cooperative learning increase academic achievement, self concept, intrinsic motivation, and prosocial behavior. In other words, children working in groups learn more and are happier doing it—and this applies to the curriculum designer as well!

Aronson (1980), using cooperative learning structures, has developed a "jigsaw" technique for enhancing group interaction and cohesiveness. The teacher using the "jigsaw" technique becomes the facilitator. The children are responsible for the curriculum. Each child is supplied a piece of information that they must research and then present to the group. Research indicates that the "jigsaw" technique increases motivation, self concept, and achievement for all children in the group. This technique is valuable for curriculum design as well.

ASSUMPTIONS FOR GROUP INTERACTION

Our approach assumes that the educational research studies just cited are critical, and, therefore, affirm the importance of group interaction in the creation of successful curriculum design. Further, this approach relies upon some humanistic statements about persons and how they work together (Gilchrist and Roberts 1974):

1. Movement toward change can begin within the present system, among the present staff.
2. It is assumed that curriculum is determined by people and that people desire to improve their work.
3. Democracy, despite its sometimes limited successes, is still the most effective means for coping with the changing demands of societies and individuals. In group process, this assumes:

    • Reliance upon consensus
    • Full and free communication
    • Encouragement of expression throughout the task-oriented activity

- Acceptance of the inevitability of conflict between organizational purposes and individual goals
- The uniqueness and dignity of the individual

4. Frameworks of structure symbolize the community within which people function. Structure facilitates; it is not an enclosure for confining people. In a community, all members have agreed to work cooperatively toward goal realization despite individual disagreements. In a community, people preserve their integrity as free thinkers and their uniqueness as individuals, yet are aware of their membership. All members are equal even though they perform different tasks.

Zander (1971, pp. 202–03) concludes:

A group's performance will be better if a number of things happen: if members are aroused to have a strong desire for group success, if each new goal is placed moderately higher than the past level of successful performance, if members are made aware that the group needs each person's best effort.

AN ORGANIZATIONAL STRATEGY

Thoughtful consideration of each step in the process of curriculum design is necessary before the actual task begins. In the past, a group was called together, and they immediately started to write curriculum. Questions of who, how many, and for how long were seldom addressed, and practical issues such as environments and rest periods for the project team were rarely discussed. This chapter deals with those not-so-trivial factors. Our strategy reflects a practical point of view, recognizing that some down-to-earth guidelines have emerged from earlier research as well as from experience with this model (Hegarty 1977).

THE SELECTION OF THE LEADER

Since responsibility for development of the actual curriculum design is shared by all participants, the leader's role is not to assume individual authorship for the final product. The leader's part in the system, however, is crucial, for he or she participates as a catalyst, an energizer, and, at times, a "whip cracker" for facilitating the work of the whole team. From the beginning, the leader sets the tone for the entire enterprise, sharing authority with participants but remaining devoted to the task of enforcing workable schedules and deadlines. The leader is a group counselor as well as a group manager.

Who should be the leader? Provided the leader assumes the role outlined in this chapter, a person from a teaching, administrative, or counseling background can be equally effective.

Frequently a curriculum design problem in a large school district presents itself from community concern or through state legislation. At that point, the office of the director of curriculum is charged with the task of producing the new materials. The director may choose to lead the development group or may choose to delegate the job to someone else. Similarly, a grassroots desire for curriculum changes may emerge from within a school, and a department chair takes the job as leader. Equally acceptable is an "outsider," a university consultant who specializes in the psychology of curriculum design or a consultant from the state department of education. For the development of training modules within a business environment, the leader could emerge from various job levels. The teacher of a college course in curriculum may assume the role of leader with his or her students. All of these persons can be successful leaders of the group. Each prospective leader must, however, understand this model of curriculum design and be willing to assume the leader role required for this method.

Understanding this model of curriculum design assumes, of course, some background in education. It specifically assumes that any leader could explain for the project team the relationships among goals, objectives, and evaluation. Leaders might have to practice the writing of goals and objectives within the framework. They also need to see the importance of each step. Most of all, they need to have a clear vision of how the process works as well as how the final product will appear.

Leaders need to be comfortable in the role required for this method. Literature on leadership shows autocratic, democratic, Rogerian, Gestalt, laissez faire roles, but this task requires a specific set of behaviors. Regardless of their precise philosophical orientation, our leaders are responsible for the process of the project and for facilitating its smooth flow. It is the leader who in concert with the group will lead discussion, block out schedules, specify work requirements, and arrange feedback sessions. It is the leader who will call the group back together. Leaders serve as "resource persons." Even though the leaders may know little about the content area or subject matter for the proposed curriculum, they do know their own responsibility: The leader is a facilitator who accepts the following principles:

- Participative decision making and internal setting of standards and goal orientations.
- Interdependence and collaboration among organizational units.
- The assumption that people are capable of exercising self-direction (Gilchrist and Roberts 1974).

THE SELECTION OF PARTICIPANTS

A graduate student may work alone or with a group to design a curriculum module. In very small curriculum design projects (e.g., two colleagues in a university seeking to restructure a course they team teach), the project team is simply defined as the two of them working together. In other small-scale projects, the participants are those affected, a "committee of the whole." In most course developments, however, there are many more individuals involved. A new set of lessons for elementary school youngsters in one city school district, for instance, is likely to affect hundreds of teachers. How then should they be included in the development stages?

Many professionals in curriculum design have assumed, for good reason, that teachers are appropriate participants for generating new materials. The teachers have the advantage of "knowing children," of a familiarity with appropriate tasks for various levels of learner performance, and of some training in writing new curriculum. Our model is based upon teachers as members of the project team. Teachers are the "experts," trained early in this model to become the decision makers.

In selecting which teachers are to participate, a number of factors are considered: institutional constraints, teacher willingness, and teacher aptitude. In initial planning, the institutional constraints must be identified to establish a framework for selection of project members. What are the budget limitations? Can teachers be freed from classroom responsibilities to work on the project on a regular basis? Can teachers be paid to work on Saturdays? What other rewards can the institution offer to participants?

In our own work in curriculum development, we have found these institutional constraints to have a crucial effect on the morale of the project team. Granted the budget limitations, each leader at the outset can, nevertheless, provide the highest possible degree of professionalism for the participants in terms of remuneration for time spent. An example is to offer a *choice* of released time from regular classrooms or extra pay for afternoon or Saturday work. Another possibility is to give "advancement unit credit" on the salary scale for participation. In university settings, the project team members can cite their role in the curriculum development as part of "university service" on their record for promotion and tenure. In all kinds of institutional structures, participants can be selected and later thanked in formal letters from the administrator in charge. Another important way to "reward" participants is recognition from peers and community through newspaper articles and in-house newsletters. Of course, in a formal class, participation is a requirement and grades are motivators.

The leader, aware of how many teachers can be selected and what can be offered them, sets about considering another major factor — aptitude. If the curriculum project at hand is to be built on an existing program, it would be wise to find those teachers who are specialists in the subject matter. If the material is new to everybody, as our solar energy material was (See Appendix A), then one might consider seeking out those teachers who possess expertise in a related field (e.g., general science). At any rate, aptitude is a valuable advantage in approaching a new subject area. Another form of aptitude, moreover, is knowledge of particular age groups of children. In selecting the team of teachers in our solar curriculum, we chose three for each grade level, K–6, specifically for their expertise in knowing what works with whom. If there are in the district teachers with particular aptitudes for curriculum design, e.g., special skill in generating instructional objectives or special skills in creating learning games, they should be considered for selection.

After the leader has appraised the widespread talent among the teachers available, thought can be given to the third selection factor—willingness. Needless to say, not every person who possesses the appropriate aptitude wants to contribute to the project team, regardless of the rewards. Such a person should be allowed to say "no," and another participant can be invited. Everybody recognizes the difference in his or her own behavior in volunteer situations from "draftee" situations. Whenever possible, then, project team members are invited to serve, allowing them the opportunity to accept or decline.

Although this model assumes a total team membership of five to thirty members, not all of them need to be teachers. Often, there are needs for special personnel to train the project team. In the case of new subject matter, frequently there is the need for an outside expert. Such an expert is expected to be present at all work sessions, with availability especially assured for the team's first training session. To use the expert's time most effectively, it is important to state what it is the development team needs to know. Under no circumstances should the expert be encouraged to "just talk to us." While the presentation might be interesting, it could well be only tangential to the project. It is advisable, rather, to be directive, to give the expert a conceptual outline for the presentation:

1. An overview of the field of study.
2. Subspecialties within the field.
3. Key concepts for learners.
4. Rationale for study, i.e., why is this subject important?

Accompanying handouts and a list of suitable bibliographic materials need to be available from the expert at the first meeting.

THE FIRST MEETING

At the initial meeting, the leader sets the tone for the entire project. Recognizing that nearly everyone feels most secure when the purpose of his or her work and role is clear, the leader needs to clearly state the project goal to be achieved—for example, a solar energy curriculum for learners in grades K–6. The leader gives background to the participants concerning how the project was planned, with special emphasis on the selection process. If the participants were chosen because they are considered to be particularly knowledgeable or able, they should be told these criteria. If they are present because of their willingness to volunteer, they should be complimented.

Since group interaction is a cornerstone of this approach, emphasis should be placed on group cohesiveness. If the participants do not know each other, "ice breaker" activities are advised. A useful idea is to have coffee or some other refreshment available at the time of arrival. If the meeting is scheduled to begin at 9:00 A.M., the preliminary agenda might read, "8:45 A.M. Welcome coffee, 9:00 A.M. Meeting." Participants who arrive early have the opportunity, then, of greeting each other comfortably over a cup of coffee, rather than standing around feeling awkward. Refreshments make things run smoother.

Whether we've been conditioned for good things occurring contiguously with good food, or if the warmth satisfies our oral needs, we can't say. We only know coffee or such helps morale. Doughnuts help too. Name tags are also useful at early meetings. If teachers represent different disciplines, it is appropriate to invite them to introduce themselves to the group, stating their names and a brief sentence about their teaching specialty. In some groups, the leader can count off dyads (two-member groups) and allow them two minutes to interview each other. Then each participant introduces his or her partner to the group.

Once all participants have been introduced, the leader shares with them the structure of the working process. The leader outlines this approach and encourages them to read Chapter 1 of this book before the next meeting. Time limits are discussed, e.g., the length of the project is stated in specific terms of number of meetings or number of weeks. The leader gives an overview of what they might expect in their training for the project, the scheduling of work sessions, and their roles as team members.

In regard to training, the leader begins by informing the team that this model is designed to serve two simultaneous purposes: to produce a set of curriculum materials and to develop a series of skills within the project team. Toward these ends, training will occur as needed, prior to each step in the process. The first training session, for instance, will involve a general view of this approach. Participants will be able to demonstrate their competency at each stage by applying what they learn to the curriculum problem at hand. The sequential steps are briefly noted again:

1. Identifying a purpose

2. Selecting designer participants
3. Selecting the content of curriculum
4. Writing goals for learners
5. Learning about instructional objectives
6. Turning goals into instructional objectives
7. Generating appropriate lessons
8. Developing instructional materials
9. Recommending a learning environment
10. Evaluating outcomes
11. Continuing feedback

The scheduling of work sessions is important to the well-being of all team members. Knowing as we do that fatigue occurs when one attempts too much learning at one session, this model follows a format which demands productivity, but in smaller workable steps. For each of the eleven steps outlined above, this procedure will be followed:

1. Background reading of specific chapter
2. Discussion of this new chapter
3. Introduction of new content material (from expert, team member responsible, or leader)
4. Introduction of new process and documentation forms
5. Subgroup work
6. Group reports
7. Evaluation

The rationale for this procedure is that psychological principles of learning are applied to facilitate the development of skills in the project members. The reading of each chapter prior to the meeting serves as a proactive facilitation or "aid" to that day's events. The discussion helps in retention of what was read.

New content, for example, poetry of the 1980s, is introduced by the participant most appropriate: either a local expert, outside expert, or a participant who has studied for this particular purpose. Then, with the new content in hand, the next process is introduced by the leader, who might say, "Now that we've read and discussed Chapter 4, 'Writing Goals for Learners,' we will write goals for our curriculum on interpersonal skills for management trainees in personnel." The leader will have appropriate forms available for that step. If the form is new, its use can be explained. In the case of goal setting, for instance, the previous group work in identifying a structure of the problem must be available to each participant.

Forms have been found to be useful in this model. They have the advantage of: setting a structure for each task, helping in expediting the completion of each task, and providing a standard of continuity between and among the products of various subgroups. Therefore, suitable forms for the various steps appear in each chapter.

The leader outlines how subgroups of the participants will work throughout the curriculum project. Tasks are specifically designed to be performed in small groups which are each responsible for a defined part of the total task. An example is a group of teachers of Head Start youngsters who divide themselves into two groups for writing behavioral objectives: one subgroup to generate objectives for three- and four-year-old learners on color identification, the other subgroup to generate objectives on concepts of shape.

After each subgroup working period, the participants return to the whole group for evaluation of each subsection. In the Head Start situation, each subgroup shares its objective with the other subgroup. Then, a contextual evaluation occurs where this present section is added to previous parts of the product.

When the leader has explored the training that participants may expect for the tasks within the development system, then the issue of how their work sessions will be scheduled is dealt with. The leader may want to share some information about attention spans and fatigue with the participants: that even intelligent adults cannot work indefinitely without breaks, and that work quality suffers in both quantity and quality when fatigue sets in.

For those reasons, activities in the curriculum design process are deliberately varied, from large group to subgroup work, and sessions always have a definite beginning and end. Time limits are not intended to be punitive; rather, they help to keep discussions task-oriented.

Each day should have an agenda. Each agenda ends with the leader and group together setting the agenda plan for the next meeting. It provides a sense of culmination—that one step has been accomplished, that the next activity will build upon the present day's work.

Breaks are important. One general rule is to plan some kind of opportunity to stop work within each ninety-minute period. It is beneficial to encourage participants to leave the work area and to relax for a short time. Food is encouraging in itself. Lunches can be fun, too. Again, though, participants should leave the work area, if possible, during lunch breaks. Groups enjoy dining together, but nobody should be pressured to join. Every person should be encouraged to spend his lunch time as he likes. The leader could suggest restaurants in the area.

At one curriculum development session where the authors were the outside consultants, the leader planned a catered lunch in the work area in the hope of maximizing opportunity to work. As it happened, the participants' behavior indicated a real desire to escape. They did fill their plates (after all, the lunch was free), but they went outside and away from the building to eat, often sitting in uncomfortable places, seemingly to avoid the work atmosphere. Eventually the authors observed that time was not saved, nor did participants work while eating. Everyone seemed to need a reasonable time totally away from his or her tasks.

At one of the working sessions using our model, the participants wanted to have a potluck buffet for a group lunch. Even though this was a good idea, in that it demonstrated a healthy group identity and high morale, it was a constant source of interruption in group tasks. Participants were busy defrosting and checking timers and slicing and serving – not writing! Our best advice is to bring a bag lunch or go out. The role of cook, host, or hostess takes the participant away from the task at hand: to develop curriculum.

Finally, at the first meeting the leader discusses each participant's role as a team member in the total process. Each participant accepts responsibility for various tasks, with opportunities for choices at each step. As a team member, one can depend upon colleagues just as the colleagues can depend upon him or her. As a decision maker, the participant has input in setting agendas, forming work groups, and evaluating products.

In one project team's effort in curriculum design (See Appendix A), the leader selected three teacher experts on each grade level, K–6, who were recommended by their subject matter district coordinators as outstanding. Although strangers at the first meeting, they developed into efficient work groups as the process continued. One example of the decision-making power of participants in this model was that subgroups used two different group process methods in achieving their tasks. After identifying goals in a large group, the subgroup of twelve teachers of kindergarten through grade three addressed the problem of how they would like to generate suitable instructional objectives for their learners, while the other nine teachers tackled the same problem for their grades, four through six.

One group felt far more comfortable as a committee of the whole, creating each objective together, while the other group split the task and performed as individuals. Both methods were successful. Both groups also maintained accountability in that they agreed to "contract" for a certain piece of the project within a time frame. The actual division of labor then was decided by the subgroup itself.

Dependence upon colleagues is necessary. Since the group frequently needs clarification in a new subject matter effort, the content expert is needed to give input to the group concerning his or her expertise. Even though the expert is available for discussion during group work, it is usually more valuable to have a written answer for future reference. It is the responsibility of the expert to have the written answers returned to the appropriate groups before the beginning of the next meeting.

The participant can count on flexibility in our curriculum design process. Even though work is specifically planned in sequential steps, alternative strategies of accomplishing those tasks are encouraged. Each step in itself is the result of the participants' roles as decision makers.

SUMMARY

This chapter addressed the role of the curriculum design team member and how the group itself functions in the process. Questions such as "Why should curriculum design be done in a group anyway?" were tackled, as well as some practical plans for organization of the team. Issues of selection of leaders and participants were examined and strategies for handling the first meeting were discussed. It was assumed that the individual participant's role in this model is one of a decision maker, responsible for his or her own part of each task and dependent upon others on the team for their participation.

FOLLOW-UP ACTIVITIES

1. State one principle of group interaction.
2. Set criteria for selecting a leader for the project team task.
3. List three topics to be discussed at the first project team meeting.
4. Role play the leader at the first meeting of the project team.
5. Write an agenda for the first meeting.
6. Make a list of materials needed for the curriculum project.

REFERENCES

Aronson, E. *The Social Animal*. San Francisco: W. H. Freeman, 1980.

Berman, P. & McLaughlin, M. *Federal Programs Supporting Educational Change*. Los Angeles: Rand Corp., 1977.

Eisner, E. *The Educational Imagination*. New York: Macmillan, 1979.

Gilchrist, R. S. & Roberts, B. R. *Curriculum Development: A Humanized Systems Approach*. Belmont, Calif.: Fearson Publishers, 1974.

Johnson, D. W. & Johnson, R. *Learning Together and Alone: Cooperation, Competition and Individuation*. Englewood Cliffs, N.J.: Prentice-Hall, 1975.

Hegarty, H. "The Problem Identification Phase of Curriculum Design." *Journal of Curriculum Studies* 1 (1977): 31–42.

Koch, R. L. & French, J. R. J., Jr. "Overcoming Resistence to Change." *Human Relations* 1 (1948): 512–33.

Lewin, K. "Group Decision and Social Change." In *Readings in Social Psychology*, rev. ed., edited by G. Swanson, T. Newcomb, & E. Hartley, 459–73. New York: Henry Holt, 1952.

Lewin, K.; Lippitt, R.; & White, R. K. "Patterns of Aggressive Behavior in Experimentally Created 'Social Climates'." *Journal of Social Psychology*, 10 (1939): 271–99.

Oliva, P. *Developing the Curriculum*. Boston: Little, Brown, 1982.

Zander, A. *Motive and Goals in Groups*. New York: Academic Press, 1971.

CHAPTER 3

SELECTING THE CONTENT OF CURRICULUM

An expert is a person who avoids the small errors while sweeping on to the grand fallacy.

Weinberg's Corollary

THE GRAND FALLACY OF EDUCATION

Whether explicit or implicit, every curriculum has emerged from some conception of structure of the content that needs to be presented. The stronger the philosophical base of the curriculum, the easier it will be to develop appropriate curriculum content. For example, a subject-centered curriculum will most likely focus on the structure of the discipline for content selection. A core curriculum is more integrated and will focus on content that revolves around social issues. Humanistic curriculum is often delineated by a needs assessment and has a focus that is personal to the learners. Unfortunately and frequently, the structural or philosophical base of curriculum content has been defined too broadly, too specifically, or, worse yet, not at all, resulting in "holes" or "gaps" in the goals and subsequent lessons. This is the grand fallacy of education: curriculum designed for everybody and nobody, leaving teachers in the classroom with shiny new lessons for their learners which demand previous knowledge or skills the learner has not yet acquired. Although it would be convenient to incorporate the exquisitely produced educational textbooks, records, and films that are available into every specific classroom curriculum, this is not possible. Teachers rightly ask, "How can they learn this when they haven't heard of that?"

This chapter addresses the crucial process of content selection for designing new curricular tasks. Content selection is essentially a map of what the curriculum will include. It is from the stated core organization of the content that goals will be chosen (See Figure 3.1). Therefore, it is crucial that the possibilities for content selection be studied and analyzed as thoroughly as possible. Questions that apply to the new learning situation need to be confronted. Why is the English curriculum being revised at the high school level? Why is a sex education curriculum being designed for sixth graders? Why are we developing a curriculum in computer education? The fundamental question to be answered is, "What is the basic structure of the content that is necessary to an understanding of this entire subject for a specific group of learners?"

Although content selection is initially overwhelming to someone who has not attempted to focus on designing curriculum, this seemingly arduous process will pay off in the long run. Lessons will relate to one another, and build upon one another. The teacher and students ultimately will meet their goals. In general, more will be accomplished because curriculum will address a specific purpose and a specific problem.

A BROAD DEFINITION OF CONTENT

Content is the basis by which learning activities are linked to each other, to goals, and to the theoretical rationale. Meaningful selection of content will involve variations from one learning situation to another, because realistically content selection must take into account the strengths and weaknesses of the teachers and of the learners. The selection of the content for any given curriculum is complex and multidimensional. It is the core organizing factor in curriculum design. McNeil (1981) states that the most common elements of curriculum organization are:

- Concepts—such as culture, growth, number, space, entropy, and evolution
- Generalization—conclusions drawn from careful observations by scientists
- Skills—proficiency plans for building continuity in programs
- Values—beliefs that are not to be questioned but are to be taken as the absolute directives of behavior

The content of any curriculum will vary depending on the concepts, principles, generalizations, theories, strategies, methods, and values. For example, an art class in early childhood education based on Piagetian theory will place a high value on cognitive growth and self expression. The concepts to be taught might include: an understanding of space, self expression, and an understanding of color. The strategy or principle of teaching might be an open-ended one

FIGURE 3.1
Selection of the Content

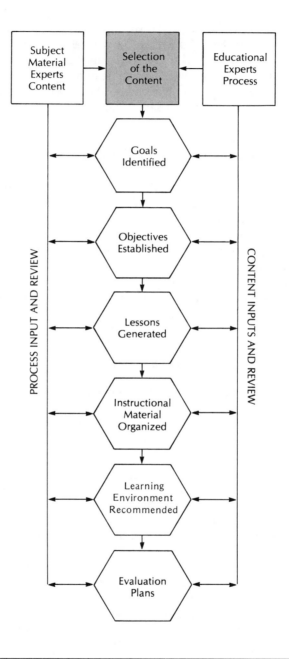

where the child is allowed the freedom to pursue his or her own intuition. The methodology would be one that places the least restrictions on the child in order to enhance self expression.

In contrast, a course in art education for early childhood based on the principle of line drawing would suggest careful attention to the drawing of objects. Concepts that would be covered might include: an understanding of space, an understanding of line qualities, an introduction to perspective. The value of the class would be to enhance aesthetic awareness. The methodology would be very directive, teaching the child how to copy objects exactly.

METHODS FOR SELECTING THE CONTENT

The following methods for selecting the content of a specific curriculum have been successfully used by the authors. Depending on the depth and complexity of the curriculum to be designed, one or two or three or all four of these methods may be necessary to select the content. Content can be developed and selected through research into the literature of that field, through the aid of an expert in that content area, through the growth of the participants into a group of new experts as a result of their own intensive purposeful study, and through a needs assessment.

Identifying Content Through Research

The project team begins its quest to select the content with an advantage if the new curriculum is to be built upon an idea already developed in some detail prior to their coming together. If there exists a written statement on the purpose of a program, like the program for gifted minors in Los Angeles, *Critical Thinking Processes* (1975) the group can begin with those documents as a starting place. Sometimes the content for a new curriculum is based in the theoretical literature, serving as a conceptual framework itself. When the Programs for the Gifted Branch of the Los Angeles Unified School District was seeking a new program in critical thinking, a theoretical article served as a beginning.

Recognizing that as far back as 1973 critical thinking was mandated as a goal of the social science program in the state, and that in 1975 the governor indicated that in addition to the traditional aims of teaching reading, writing, and arithmetic, the public schools of the state were to stress learning to think effectively, a curriculum committee in Los Angeles set about developing suitable materials. Since it was clearly a problem in designing a new curriculum "from scratch," the project team searched the research literature for help in establishing some core concepts for what belonged in the content of a critical thinking course.

Project team members decided that among the articles they identified there was one essay that could serve as a comprehensive point of departure for their work, "A Concept of Critical Thinking" by Robert E. Ennis (1962). Ennis defined critical thinking as "the correct assessing of statements," listing twelve aspects of critical thinking:

1. Grasping the meaning of a statement.
2. Judging whether there is ambiguity in a line of reasoning.
3. Judging whether certain statements contradict each other.
4. Judging whether a conclusion follows necessarily.
5. Judging whether a statement is specific enough.
6. Judging whether a statement is actually the application of a certain principle.
7. Judging whether an observation statement is reliable.
8. Judging whether an inductive conclusion is warranted.
9. Judging whether the problem has been identified.
10. Judging whether something is an assumption.
11. Judging whether a definition is adequate.
12. Judging whether a statement made by an alleged authority is adequate.

These aspects of critical thinking, then, became the core organizing concepts for the group's future work in selecting the content. Goals later reflected the twelve aspects of critical thinking, and objectives were stated to achieve those goals (Los Angeles City Schools, 1975).

Identifying Content with an Expert

A second method for selecting content is to ask an expert in the field. Often a project team must break new ground, writing curriculum in brand new subject areas where the material is unfamiliar. When this is the case, an expert can give valuable information to the participants, saving hours and hours of research time. The expert has the advantage of a wider view of the topic area and its interrelationships.

The choice of the "right" expert is critical and should be based on the needs of the group the curriculum will be planned for. If the curriculum will serve elementary school children, then the expert must have a background in learner characteristics in elementary school children. Experience in working with teachers and children is essential. An expert who only knows the subject matter, with no idea of how to present it to others or work in a group, may be counterproductive.

In the solar energy curriculum (See Appendix A) the group took expert advice in selecting the content of the curriculum. As a result of initial input from the outside expert, the participants identified some key concepts required for an understanding of solar energy. The group began with a brainstorming session listing crucial concept areas. They listed fundamental questions as well: What is the sun? How does it work? What is energy? What is solar energy? Why is there an energy crisis? Why solar?

Those logical background concepts were easily identified. Others were more difficult to grasp. Some participants thought that identifying different kinds of energy would be important, while others said that modes of technological solutions to energy problems should take precedence in the conceptual framework. Many members of the project team asserted that "quality of life" issues should be stressed most.

At that point the expert began to earn his consultant fee in earnest. He showed how all of the expressed concerns could fit compatibly within a conceptual framework. He agreed that the ideas of the sun and of energy were the foundation, but solar energy itself needed to be identified as a content area. Within that concept was the question, "How can solar energy be used effectively?" Then the technological possibilities could become concept areas of their own—for example, passive modes, active modes, and indirect modes. All of these, finally, create implications for the last concept area, the quality of life issues. The model emerged with seven key areas for content development (See Figure 3.2.).

Identifying Content by the Participants

A third method for delineating a suitable content of the problem is for the participants to become experts in the new field. They can research what already exists and they can interview experts, but finally they will be the sole decision makers in selecting the content. They do not have the advantage of building from a theoretician like Ennis in critical thinking or from an outside expert, as in the solar energy curriculum. This is a case of the project team's trusting its own judgment from the evidence they gather. Often this approach is necessary when theories and experts are not available.

Peace Corps teacher training is a real-life example of this method of selecting the content for curriculum development. A small project team, charged with the task of preparing suitable curriculum materials for inservice training for Peace Corps volunteers engaged in teaching in Western Samoa, went about identifying the basic concept areas that must be included in the framework (Wulf 1979). One strategy was to look carefully at the "givens"—that is, the stated purpose for the new curriculum, the mission of the project. Another useful effort was to study preliminary data from in-country staff regarding what they appraised to be the most important conceptual areas. Since one of the project team members was an expert in teacher training, she addressed the question of what key areas of content were deemed necessary for Peace Corps teachers in this par-

FIGURE 3.2
Selection of the Content

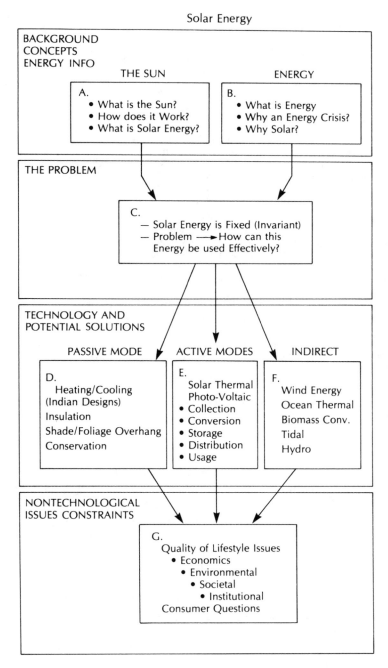

Solar Energy

BACKGROUND
CONCEPTS
ENERGY INFO

THE SUN   ENERGY

A.
• What is the Sun?
• How does it Work?
• What is Solar Energy?

B.
• What is Energy
• Why an Energy Crisis?
• Why Solar?

THE PROBLEM

C.
— Solar Energy is Fixed (Invariant)
— Problem ——▶ How can this
Energy be used Effectively?

TECHNOLOGY AND
POTENTIAL SOLUTIONS

PASSIVE MODE   ACTIVE MODES   INDIRECT

D.
Heating/Cooling
(Indian Designs)
Insulation
Shade/Foliage Overhang
Conservation

E.
Solar Thermal
Photo-Voltaic
• Collection
• Conversion
• Storage
• Distribution
• Usage

F.
Wind Energy
Ocean Thermal
Biomass Conv.
Tidal
Hydro

NONTECHNOLOGICAL
ISSUES CONSTRAINTS

G.
Quality of Lifestyle Issues
• Economics
• Environmental
• Societal
• Institutional
Consumer Questions

FIGURE 3.3
Steps Involved in the Needs Assessment Process

The steps proposed for conducting a school's needs assessment are:

1. Identify the student-oriented goals.
2. Rank the importance of these goals without regard to performance levels.
3. Assess the level of performance for each of the goals.
4. Establish a priority for each student goal, considering both importance and performance.

Step 1: Identify the student-oriented goals (content areas).

Programs under the Consolidated Application require the following student components: language development, reading, mathematics, multicultural education, health and auxiliary services. Goals should be developed within each component as a first step so that project staff can initially focus on the basic elements of the program.

Step 2: Rank the importance of the goals.*

Each group deemed significant to the planning process ranks the student goals in order of importance. It is not likely that equal attention will be needed or can be given to all areas. To keep the process simple, yet moving steadily toward the desired outcome, the importance of each goal is considered *without regard to current performance level;* e.g., a school might have very high reading scores but still consider mastery of basic reading skills a high importance goal.

Step 3: Assess the level of performance for each of the goals.

Data are collected to identify how well students are performing in each goal area. The data should come from the best available source. For example, a profile of each student in reading or math, including a record of skill mastery, provides a far better source of information than does a questionnaire calling for teacher estimates of mastery. A general rule of thumb is to use those available data which stand the best chance of being accurate. The performance level for each goal is categorized as high, moderate, or low.

Step 4: Establish a priority for each student goal, considering both importance and performance.

ticular environment. Another team member researched the major topic of the cultural differences between the community's expectations of teachers in the United States and in Western Samoa. The thinking of the project team resulted in the following list of concepts:

1. The psychology of teaching.
2. The Samoan student in the New Zealand educational system.
3. The problem of teaching effectively in Western Samoa.
4. Appropriate cross-cultural methodology for classroom management.
5. Appropriate methodology for instruction.

These concepts became the core organizers for the entire curriculum for inservice teacher training for Peace Corps in Western Samoa. They were developed by teamwork!

The goals are placed into one of the nine cells provided in the figure below. Priorities are established, high to low, from upper left to lower right, with cell #1 being top priority. Cells numbered 2 have second-level priority; cells numbered 3 are third level; and cells 4 and 5 have least priority.

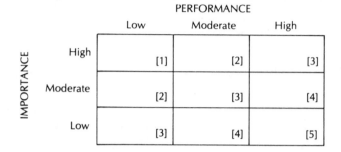

The technique used for displaying the data is based on the following premises:

1. Findings of a needs assessment, in order to be useful, *must* establish priorities.
2. Performance level and importance of the goal share equally in determining priorities.
3. Data are not useful unless the users understand, accept, and can *act* upon the information.

---

*This is not required to complete the Consolidated Application, but is a significant step for a needs assessment.

Identifying Content Through Needs Assessment

In the area where no curriculum has existed before, a project team is often overwhelmed with the question, "Where do we start?" A reasonable beginning is to study the overall purpose of the project as it was explained to the participants when they were recruited to the team, and then to conduct a needs assessment.

A needs assessment can be the most democratic way to select the content (See Figure 3.3.). A needs assessment gives the curriculum personal relevance for the participants. It is a public process of interviewing teachers, administrators, experts, parents, students, politicians, and community leaders about how they would attack the problem that needs to be solved. After collecting information from all of these groups, the consensus is determined, values are listed in priority, and important aspects of the content are specified.

For example, in developing an infant-parent program for a low

FIGURE 3.4
Infant–Toddler Program

PARENT QUESTIONNAIRE

1.   Name of child_____

2.   Age of child _____

3.   Number of children in family _____

4.   Is this your first, second, third child? _____

5.   Mother's occupation _____

6.   Father's occupation_____

7.   Child's health _____

       _____ Excellent   _____ Average   _____ Poor

8.   Child's last physical examination _____
     _____

9.   Which *two* words out of the following would you use to describe your child:

       _____ Active   _____ Anxious   _____ Aggressive

       _____ Very active   _____ Even-tempered   _____ Contented/happy

       _____ Passive

10. Do you have any concerns about your child's sleeping patterns? If yes, what are
     they?
     _____
     _____

11. Do you have any concerns about your child's eating habits? If yes, what are they?
     _____

socioeconomic multicultural preschool, one group took into consideration the opinions of teachers, administrators, health educators,
research specialists, and parents; and the observable behaviors of
families. The following terms, elicited from these opinions, became
the focus of the new curriculum:

1. Nutrition.
2. Medical and dental care.
3. Separation issues.
4. Day care/child care.
5. Family planning.
6. Language acquisition.
7. Cognitive development.
8. Social development.
9. The physical environment for the infant.

These nine concepts served as the basis for another needs assessment with the participants in the infant-parent program. The in-

12. Do your children get along well with each other? _____

     Describe their interactions_____

13. How does your child react when you leave him with others?
     _____ HAPPY   _____ ANGRY   _____ SAD

14. Does your child play well with other children?
     _____

15. Do you have a hard time handling your child? If yes, how?
     _____
     _____

16. Do you feel that your child is developing at a normal rate in terms of physical,
     emotional, and mental growth?
     _____
     _____

17. Does your child talk? _____
     _____

18. At what age did your child start to crawl?_____
     _____

19. Can your child walk yet? _____
     _____

structor interviewed each parent who expressed an interest in the program (See Figure 3.4.). The curriculum was based on the expressed needs of the parents, the opinions of authorities in the community, and the opinions of the school staff.

THE CONTENT AS AN ORGANIZER

Once the content has been identified by the team and classified into an appropriate order, each concept area can be assigned an identity. These can be simple numbers or letters, e.g., in the critical thinking curriculum each aspect received a number; "Grasping the meaning of a Statement" emerged as Concept Area 1. In the solar energy structure "The Sun" became Concept Area A. These serve as groundwork for easy future reference to specific parts of the curriculum. Concept Area A in the solar energy curriculum is born in the goal setting phase, but it retains its identity through objective writing, lesson development, and evaluation (See Appendix A).

THE CONTENT AS AN ASSESSMENT OF "NEED TO KNOW"

Frequently a project team successfully uses an outside expert in selecting their content but subsequently finds there are great gaps in the team's own knowledge. Our model provides for the necessary training at this point—before the team members need to use their familiarity with the framework in creating objectives and lessons.

The subject matter expert (or most able team member) takes responsibility for the following training. Since the expert's initial presentation (as outlined in Chapter 2) included an overview of the field of study, a summary of subspecialties within the field, some key concepts for learners, and a rationale for study, the participants already have some introduction. At this point some depth consideration of the content area identified is important. Time is allocated for a whole group presentation by the expert. The presentation, or series of presentations, should be exhaustive in that all major areas are discussed. The expert can use any suitable materials for this training, e.g., films, filmstrips, tapes, books, lectures, etc., always keeping in mind the needs and preferences of the project team.

THE CONTENT AND ITS LIMITS

The content once selected can be amended. However, it serves in its final form as a statement of the conceptual scope of the curriculum. In the case of the major concept areas for the Peace Corps teacher trainees, for instance, the participants can be assured that a peripheral topic (e.g., the history of the Samoan language) is not part of this curricular effort. In common sense terms, one might say that the content selected stakes out the extent of the forest and identifies the main trees.

Sometimes new input calls for adding to the selected content. This is easily accomplished at this present step through group discussion. In selecting the content for the solar energy curriculum using the expert approach, the participants decided after training that they needed one more topic: the scientific method. Since this body of knowledge seemed to the team to be prerequisite to other concepts, the scientific method was given a high priority in the already-established content areas.

SUMMARY

This chapter broadly defined the meaning of "content." It addressed the process of selecting the content which serves as a foundation for the future stages of lesson developing and evaluation. Four methods—research, input from experts in the particular field, input from the participants themselves, and needs assessment—were outlined with real-life examples. The functions of the resultant structural framework were to provide core organization, to highlight areas where the team needed more preparation, and to set parameters for the project's scope and the change that might be needed.

FOLLOW-UP ACTIVITIES

1. Choose one of the four methods for selecting the content and list three procedures that would be part of that method.
2. Select a content area for a curriculum of your choice.
3. Show two ways of showing a structure graphically. (We have shown the diagram in Figure 3.2, as well as lists of key concepts.) What new ways might be more effective?
4. Compare four methods for selecting content.
5. Explain how an expert should be used on a project team.
6. In your own words, explain the significance of selecting the content in curriculum design.

REFERENCES

Cox, J. *The Needs Assessment: A Guide for School Level Activities.* Downey, Calif: Office of the Los Angeles County Superintendent of Schools, 1979.

Eisner, E. *The Educational Imagination.* New York: Macmillan, 1979.

Ennis, R. E. "A Concept of Critical Thinking." *Harvard Educational Review* 32, 1 (1962): 157–87.

Lampert, S.; Wulf, K.; & Yanow, G. "A Solar Energy Curriculum for Elementary Schools," University of Southern California Progress Report, No. 1–EY–76–5–03–113.

Los Angeles City Schools Instructional Planning Division, Programs for Gifted Section, *Critical Thinking Processes,* 1975.

McNeil, J. *Curriculum: A Comprehensive Introduction.* Boston: Little, Brown, 1981.

Wulf, K. M. "A Humanistic Approach to In-Service Training for Peace Corps Teachers." Paper read at Eighty-Seventh Annual Convention of the American Psychological Association, 1979.

CHAPTER 4

WRITING GOALS FOR LEARNERS

Whenever you set out to do something, something else must be done first.
Murphy's Law

Goals are a structural part of curriculum planning. Goals emerge from a point of view or a platform (Leithwood 1981). For example, such underlying views of schooling as the development of cognitive process, curriculum as technology, self actualization, social reconstructionism, personal relevance, or academic rationalism may serve as the focus of the curriculum (Eisner 1979). Goals or platforms reflect the philosophy and values of their writers; their variations are as broad as curriculum itself.

The most famous of all statements on the purpose and nature of schooling are the Seven Cardinal Principles of Secondary Education written in 1918. Broad goals in the areas of health, general knowledge, family life, vocation, civic education, ethical character, and worthy leisure time were established for the nation. These set the foundation for subsequent educational goals, which were generally recognized to have dual purposes: to prepare individuals to be productive members of society and to enable individuals to develop their own potential (Saylor, Alexander, & Lewis 1981).

Since goals are general rather than specific, their major purpose is to indicate the desired direction of curriculum. With the widespread movement for measurement of competency in education in the last twenty years, goals are receiving more attention. In our approach, goals are essential to move the curriculum development from the selection of the content to the actual instructional objectives.

According to Zais (1976), an educational goal differs from an aim and an objective. *Aims* are "life outcomes, targets removed from the school situation to such an extent that their achievement is determinable only in that part of life well after the completion of school" (p. 299). *Goals* are "school outcomes," reflecting long-range, general effects. *Objectives* are specific learning outcomes as a result of classroom instruction.

Since goals are statements of a broad direction or general intent, they are not concerned with a particular achievement within a specified time period. However, general educational goals should not be so broad as to be unrealistic. Goals should be adopted that are appropriate to the total learning environment.

In our approach, it is suggested that team members locate any existent goals for their area of concern, as they will aid in establishing a point of view. The major concern of goal writing, in this chapter, is the work that the project team accomplishes in direct response to the selection of the content explained in the previous chapter. The task is then to take each content area, with its letter label, and write suitable goals (See Figure 4.1).

STAGES IN GOAL WRITING

There are three stages to goal writing. First, the participants must be trained in goal writing. Second, the team members must be assigned to specific content areas. Third, the resultant goals must be evaluated by the entire group.

Training in Goal Writing

Since many of the project team members may have a background in goal writing, this training session may be brief. Its main function is to serve as a collective opportunity to agree upon definitions and form. It is useful for the group to recognize that goals and objectives are two distinct steps in our model, and that this step involves goals only. Thus, the emphasis should be on goals as general statements of purpose for the new curriculum.

The group might agree to a definition of a goal such as "a statement of broad direction or intent which is general and timeless and is not concerned with a particular achievement within a specified time period" (Plakos 1976). The group could also prepare its own definition of a goal. The chief criteria, however, are that all members agree that the goals they write will be: broad in scope, general statements of purpose, and long-term or far-reaching.

There are three points of view that can be taken when writing goals: student, teacher, and curriculum. Two examples of goals written from the student's point of view are: to develop an appreciation of the fine arts and to create an understanding of the values of various

FIGURE 4.1
Goals Identified

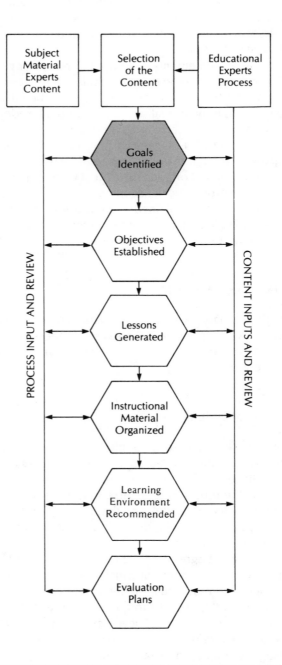

cultures. Examples of goals written from the teacher's point of view are: to individualize instruction and to assess affective behavior (Shane & Weaver 1980). Goals phrased as the aims or intents of a curriculum can be illustrated by this example of a program in graduate education for mental health professionals:

> The intention of this curriculum is to: 1) facilitate the delivery of mental health service to individuals and groups in the designated catchment area; 2) create a mosaic of specialized professional orientation—a new generalist; 3) search for and discover general substantive and methodological guides which transcend differences, both personal and professional. A major attempt at curriculum reform, it is a bold and deliberate step to 4) refresh and rejuvenate the world of study, learning, teaching and delivering a human service in the form of therapeusis and consultation. (Garner 1972)

The group will decide which format of goal writing is most appropriate for the task. Goals, for instance, can be a full sentence, e.g., "The student appreciates music," or a fragment, e.g., "appreciation of music." The following guidelines aid in stating appropriate goals:

1. Educational goals should describe the desired product. The units that will be offered, the instructional methodologies, and the environmental conditions for learning should be determined later in the development process. Educational goals identify in general terms what the student will be like as a result of education.
2. Educational goals should be stated as desirable characteristics attributable to learning.
3. Goals should define what each individual is expected to derive.
4. The scope of educational goals is important. Goals should not be so broad that they give purpose and justification to anything. Conversely, goals should not be as narrow as behavioral objectives (Johnson 1972).

Teamwork

After common definitions and format for goal statements have been mutually established by the entire group, the team members return to their own tasks. They prepare goals for the project that are comprehensive and exhaustive. All goals are derived from the concept area identified in the last stage of work, the development of a structure.

In the example on curricula for solar energy for elementary school (See Chapter 3), the structure in each case served as the foundation for goal setting. Frequently, it is found that one major concept area serves as parent for many goals (See Figure 4.2). Clearly, in order

FIGURE 4.2
Goal Statements for Solar Energy

z.1   The students grow in their ability to apply the scientific method.

A.1   The students understand that the sun is essential to all life on earth.
A.2   The students learn the physical properties of the sun.
A.3   The students learn the astronomical relationships of the sun to the earth.
A.4   The students learn that all of our sources of energy on earth are traceable to the sun.

B.1   The students learn to recognize various forms of energy.
B.2   The students evolve a concept of energy.
B.3   The students understand the difference between renewable and nonrenewable energy sources. (Clean/renewable is desirable and environmentally sound.)
B.4   The students learn about energy measurements.
B.5   The students understand how the present "energy crisis" is a crisis in the way we use energy.
B.6   The students know about alternative energy sources.
B.7   The students understand energy conservation.

C.1   The students understand the basic problems involved in utilizing solar energy.

D.1   The students learn some of the ways of using solar energy (Passive/Active–Direct/Indirect) (Matrix).
D.2   The students understand some of the technical problems involved in utilizing solar energy: collection (and noncollection-passive) conversion, utilization, storage.

G.1   The students recognize how political issues affect solar energy technology.
G.2   The students understand how economic issues affect solar energy.
G.3   The students understand the environmental impact of solar energy.
G.4   The students understand the sociological constraints on using solar energy.
G.5   The students understand the institutional constraints on using solar energy.

to develop the major idea within the structure it is advisable to write as many goals as needed.

For the solar energy curriculum, the seven concept areas served as a foundation for nineteen expressed goals, each coded with a letter label of concept area from the selection of the content and then numbered as a set within the major area. All concepts are developed into appropriate goals.

There was an addition to the goals for the solar energy curriculum that did not appear originally. One new goal was added after the initial creation of the structure of the content. The new goal – growth in the ability to apply the scientific method – was regarded by the participants as a necessary concomitant to the other goals. Adding a new goal at this point allows for its future development into objectives, lessons, and evaluation.

The project team makes its own decision regarding the staffing of the goal-writing groups. The participants can deploy themselves in a variety of ways: small groups can deal with separate concept areas, individual members can each write goals for one concept, or all can work as a whole. As most curriculum developers have more goals than the number of basic concepts in their structural framework, it is often more efficient, particularly in larger teams (fifteen or more participants), to break into smaller groups and to divide the task. In the solar energy example, the twenty-five-member team assigned themselves to groups of three or four to write goals for each of their seven concept areas. Then they were able to offer evaluation and feedback to the other small groups when all goals were assembled for the final statement.

Evaluation by the Team

With the structure of the goal areas before them, the team members report to the whole group on the results of the goal writing. Each goal is evaluated in terms of both form and content. To help in assessing the quality of the written objective, a checklist (See Figure 4.3) for evaluating program goals is useful (Gronlund 1978). As for content, the participants give feedback as to whether the goals, as written, actually develop the intent of the concept areas. Questions such as "Do we have all the goals we need?" and "Can some of our goals be combined?" are discussed. Finally, each numbered goal must be classified in the most appropriate logical order within its concept area in the structure of the content.

A STATEMENT OF RATIONALE

When the project team has accepted the goals for form, content, and logical order, the members will probably want to use them to write a concise statement of rationale for the entire project. Building upon the purpose for the new curriculum design already established prior to their meeting together, the members can now use the structure they developed, complete with appropriate goals. A short rationale serves to tell: whom the new curriculum is for, why it is needed, and what the students will be like as a result of having experienced it. The rationale is a written justification for the curriculum.

As an example, this formal statement of rationale emerged from the goal writing sessions of the solar energy curriculum project:

> In view of accelerated depletion of "conventional" energy sources, there is a need to educate our society in the use and conservation of these dwindling resources. Not only will our present lifestyles be affected, but also those of future generations. Therefore, there is a concomitant need for development and implementation of alternative energy sources, primarily of solar energy.
>
> Since students now in elementary schools will be the sector of the world's population most directly affected by problems of energy deple-

FIGURE 4.3
Checklist for Evaluating Program Goals

PROGRAM GOALS

DEFINITION: A goal is a statement of broad intent which is general and timeless and
not concerned with a particular achievement within a specified time period. Each goal
should be stated:

    a.   At a level of generality that clearly indicates the expected learning outcome
and that is readily definable by specific types of student behavior.

    b.   So that it includes only one general learning outcome rather than a combina-
tion of several outcomes.

    c.   In terms of student performance rather than teacher performance.

    d.   As a learning product rather than in terms of the learning process.

(Gronlund, pp. 7–11)

		Yes	No
1.	Is each goal stated at the proper level of generality? Does it clearly indicate learning outcome? Is it readily definable by specific objectives?	_____	_____
2.	Does each goal include only one general learning outcome?	_____	_____
3.	Is each goal stated in terms of student performance, not teacher performance?	_____	_____
4.	Is each goal stated as a learning product, not process?	_____	_____

COMMENTS:

---

*tion, it is appropriate immediately to provide them with programs dealing
with concepts of solar energy. This curriculum, then, aims to educate
children in grades kindergarten through six toward two major goals: 1) an
appreciation of the need for energy conservation, and 2) an understanding
of the potential of the sun as a suitable alternative energy resource
(Lampert, Wulf, & Yanow, 1975, p. 1).*

SUMMARY

This chapter discussed goal writing, which is based on the selection
of the content created by the team in its earlier work sessions. Three
stages to goal writing were outlined with illustrative examples: training in goal writing, teamwork in producing goals for specific idea

areas, and evaluation of the resultant goals. The chapter concluded with suggestions on writing a brief rationale from the goals.

FOLLOW-UP ACTIVITIES

1. Explain how a goal is different from an instructional objective.
2. Write at least one goal for each concept area from a selection of the content.
3. Create a plan for allocating team members to the task of writing goals for eight established idea areas.
4. Evaluate three goals in terms of form and content.
5. Write a rationale for a new curriculum that is *outside* your field of specialty.

REFERENCES

Eisner, E. *The Educational Imagination* New York: Macmillan, 1979.

Garner, G. S. "Considerations in Building a Curriculum: A Systems Approach." Paper presented at the American Personnel and Guidance Association Annual Meeting, 1972.

Gronlund, N. E. *Stating Behavioral Objectives for Classroom Instruction. 2d ed.* London: Macmillan, 1978.

Johnson, M. "Stating Educational Goals: Some Issues and a Proposal." A background paper prepared for the New York State Commission on the Quality, Cost, and Financing of Elementary and Secondary Education, Albany, New York: State University of New York at Albany, 1972. Mimeo.

Lampert, S.; Wulf, K.; & Yanow, G. "A Solar Energy Curriculum for Elementary Schools," University of Southern California. Progress Report No. 1–EY–76–5–03–0113.

Leithwood, K. "The Dimensions of Curriculum Innovation" *Journal of Curriculum Studies* 13 (1981): 45–60.

Plakos, J.; Plakos, M. E.; & Babcock, R. W. "Developing Useful Objectives." California Evaluation Improvement Project. San Mateo County Evaluation Improvement Center, 1976.

Saylor, J. G.; Alexander, W. A.; & Lewis, A. J. *Curriculum Planning for Better Teaching and Learning,* 4th ed. New York: Holt, Rinehart, & Winston, 1981.

Shane, H., & Weaver, R. *Curriculum Planning for a Society in Transition.* New York: Holt, Rinehart, & Winston, 1980.

Zais, R. S. *Curriculum: Principles and Foundations,* New York: Thomas Y. Crowell, 1976.

CHAPTER 5

MASTERING INSTRUCTIONAL OBJECTIVES

If it looks easy, it's tough.

Stockmeyer's Theorem

The history of instructional objectives indicates a dramatic impact upon thinking among educators in the past sixty years. In the early 1900s, Franklin Bobbitt advocated writing objectives for organizing curriculum, arguing for "activity analysis" which examined the activities people engage in as they live their daily lives. He described in *The Curriculum* (1918, p. 42):

> *Human life, however varied, consists in the performance of specific activities. Education that prepares one for life is one that prepares definitely and adequately for these specific activities. However numerous and diverse they may be for any social class, they can be discovered. This requires only that one go out into the world of affairs and discover the particulars of which these affairs consist. These will show the abilities, attitudes, habits, appreciations, and forms of knowledge that men need. These will be the objectives of the curriculum. They will be numerous, definite, and particularized. The curriculum will then be that series of experiences which children and youth must have by way of attaining those objectives.*

After 1920, Bobbitt was joined by W. W. Charters and David Snedden, both advocates of curriculum organization based on behavioral objectives. Like Bobbitt, Charters studied behavior, but limited his attention to tasks adults performed during work. In *Curriculum Construction* (1923), he outlined the procedure used to write objectives:

1. Identify objectives
2. Select ideals
3. Arrange ideals according to significance
4. Construct activities in order of value
5. Select those activities of highest value
6. Gather illustrations in appropriate instructional order

David Snedden, a sociologist, attempted to match specific kinds of work to the learner's ability. He suggested in *Sociological Determination of Objectives in Education* (1921) that "case groups" (large classifications of learners who shared similar abilities and interests) be matched with appropriate objectives. Snedden reduced his objectives into smaller objective units, *peths*. These peths were reassembled into *strands* (categories for the activities performed as an adult). Through organization of the curriculum into separate little units of work, Snedden hoped to provide an efficient assembly line model for facilitating the movement of learners through the school curriculum to life as adults.

Ralph Tyler continued the tradition of concentrating on behavior when developing curriculum. In *Basic Principles of Curriculum and Instruction* (1949), he proposed stating objectives in terms which identify the kind of behavior to be developed in the student as well as the content or area of life in which the behavior will operate. Objectives might assume different emphasis: a statement of what the teacher intends to do, a list of topics or concepts to be covered in a course, or a change of learner behavior.

The most recent theorists developing detailed formats for the writing of instructional objectives — Mager (1975), Gronlund (1978), and Gagné and Briggs (1974) — stress the importance of precisely stated behavioral components systematically linked to the goals and structure of curriculum. These ideas form the theoretical framework for the approach suggested in this book.

ADVANTAGES OF INSTRUCTIONAL OBJECTIVES TO SCHOOLS

In developing curriculum, instructional objectives are required for four fundmental reasons: for instructional gains, for longitudinal validation of school effectiveness, to assess the cost effectiveness of educational programs, and for an individualized instructional program which relies on a detailed, carefully sequenced set of objectives. The following paragraphs will expand upon this reasoning.

Instructional Gains

First, the objectives for an instructional program must be stated in terms of instructional outcomes. These outcomes are stated as behaviors. Without them there is little basis for deciding which learning intervention or teaching strategy would be most effective. When decisions on the selection of teaching strategies are made without objectives, there are no empirical means of determining the degree of their effectiveness. "It is doubtless true that most decisions about changes in instructional practice are made without verification in terms of what someone thinks is the effect of the practice on what is hoped to be the result. Consequently, systematic program revisions are virtually precluded in the absence of measurable performance objectives" (Bushnell 1970).

Longitudinal Validation

A second reason for instructional objectives is the need for longitudinal validation of the effectiveness of schooling in helping young people cope with their social and economic environment after they leave school. If a student's behavioral attainment for entering the adult world is unknown, there is little basis for attributing the youngster's success or lack of it to the school experience. The selection of certain sets of instructional objectives is strictly a matter of choice. Decision makers at the national, state, or local level must judge one objective to be important and reasonable, while others are not. One critical criterion for the selection of objectives is that they appear to relate to preparing a youngster for his or her role in the school environment. Such objectives tend to be selected in terms of their face value. However, face validity is often misleading, and the appearance of relevance may not be supported by empirical evidence. Revisions in educational goals as a result of follow-up studies of students can become a widespread practice.

Cost Effectiveness

A third reason for requiring instructional objectives is the need to assess the cost effectiveness of educational programs. In the wake of reduced funding for education (e.g., the Proposition 13 mandate by Californians in 1978), it is apparent that taxpayers have grown tired of increased taxation for education with no tangible evidence of the effect of these expenditures. With a more precise behavioral statement, it will more likely be possible to associate behavior change with program costs. Student learning could become the main, if not the only, basis upon which cost effectiveness analyses are made.

Individualized Instruction

Finally, another advantage of instructional objectives is the reliance of an individualized program on detailed, carefully sequenced sets of objectives. If schools are ever to reach their goal of tailoring learning experiences to an individual student's needs, then this step-by-step progress in mastering an instructional sequence must be measurable for validation.

ADVANTAGES OF INSTRUCTIONAL OBJECTIVES FOR TEACHERS AND STUDENTS

Like society in general, teachers and students benefit from the use of instructional objectives in the classroom through their knowledge of the task, through the possibilities for evaluation, and through the opportunities for preparing appropriate materials. This process attempts to increase educational effectiveness by clarifying educational objectives with great precision, and then by redesigning the entire educational process in order to ensure student achievement of these objectives.

Why state the curriculum objectives in terms of anticipated change in student behavior? In the first place, both the student and the teacher know exactly what is expected from completion of an instructional unit. There are no unexpected or surprise results since both parties have agreed upon the end product. Similarly, more accurate evaluation of the student's achievement can occur. The student is assured that such evaluation will always reflect the skills, knowledge, and concepts developed through the materials with the assistance of the teacher. Clearly written objectives, when reworded, produce ready-made test items (See Figure 5.1). Without a doubt, more appropriate instructional materials and teaching strategies can be selected to ensure achievement of the stated objectives. In order for this to be done well, the objectives must be specific and unambiguous.

OPPOSITION TO INSTRUCTIONAL OBJECTIVES

Objections to instructional objectives have been voiced by critics within and outside education. The behavioral objectives movement of the 1960s, in retrospect, is now associated with too many curriculum failures, e.g., bits and pieces of information, limited generality, and learner inability to integrate and apply information. Some denounce instructional objectives for practical reasons: they are tedious and difficult to write, and their ultimate value is not worth the effort it takes to state them. Users respond, however, that once objectives are written, they can be used repeatedly, making the effort worthwhile.

FIGURE 5.1
The Relationship Between Objectives and Instructional Materials

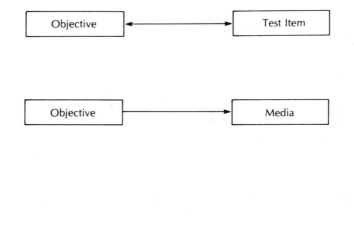

(Cyrs and Lowenthal, 1970)

Others complain that instructional objectives ignore the more subjective dimensions of human experience. According to one dissenter, "Some unmeasurables are immeasurably important." This complaint is not valid in our approach, since instructional objectives are dependent upon the content and goals already identified as important. Thus, instructional objectives give direction to the curriculum.

Another concern about instructional objectives is that they deal with measurable behavior, forcing the teacher to teach to the measurables and stressing the more observable, quantitative, and replicative material. While some objectives can be written at higher levels of application, analysis, and synthesis, these objectives are more difficult to achieve and have not been the central concern of curriculum design. In the past, instruction has been limited to lower levels of cognitive functioning.

Instructional objectives reflect a problem in definition in that a concept is defined in terms of the operations by which it is measured. Furthermore, measurement theory encourages multiple measures of a concept. This is a successful approach in the physical world where concepts like *space* or *density* can be precisely measured in more than one way. Applying these principles to human behavior, however, is vastly more difficult where concepts like *intelligence, learning,* or *self concept* are involved. *Intelligence,* for example, is defined operationally as simply a score on a specific test. If other independent measures of intelligence are attempted, they will not agree perfectly, owing to problems of test reliability and validity. This suggests to some critics that there are as many kinds of intelligence as there are ways to measure it. This problem underscores an important caution: just because a concept can be measured in behavioral terms, there is no guarantee it therefore exists in any significant or fruitful way (Isaac & Michael 1977).

Another criticism is that instructional objectives reflect an "overconcern" with measurement. Whereas a long-term principle in educational psychology has been that when anything exists in some amount, it can be measured, critics of objectives accuse believers of operating on the converse of that statement: "If you can't measure it, it doesn't exist." Thus, advocates of instructional objectives are dismissed as simplistic "bean counters."

A final complaint against instructional objectives is that there are some forms of knowledge that are truly unmeasurable—"tacit knowledge" that underlies an individual's skill or competence in real-world problem solving. This form of learning may well be beyond measurement using the instruments available today.

THE PURPOSE OF INSTRUCTIONAL OBJECTIVES

One might think that all of the battles over instructional objectives have been fought. They have not. Widely advocated in the 1960s and 1970s as the methodology of educational science, the behavioral objectives movement held great promise. Proponents argued that objectives would help keep instruction task-oriented and measurable. Opponents accused them of reducing all student learning to tiny inconsequential bits of behavior. It is fair to say that both groups could supply enormous amounts of data to support their views.

The real issue, now, is not whether to have objectives or not. Indeed, every teacher has objectives, even if they are not verbalized or written into appropriate form. The real issue is how instructional objectives fit into curriculum development and how they can be used most effectively.

Early curriculum written from instructional objectives was criticized as being only that—simply a list of objectives and accompanying tests for mastery of those objectives. Sometimes the origin of those objectives was not clear, and some critics suspected that only the easily written "instructional" parts of the new curriculum were included. Our approach assumes that, contrary to early practices, curriculum never emerges directly from the instructional objective;

FIGURE 5.2
Objectives Established

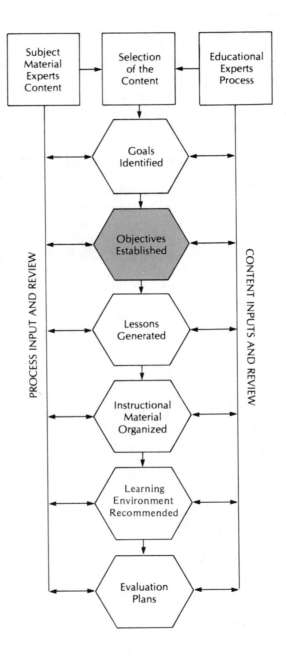

rather, the objective is a logical outgrowth of the structural framework and of the stated goals. Instructional objectives here are not the beginning or the end of the curriculum, but rather a process by which goals are translated into appropriate lessons (See Figure 5.2).

CHARACTERISTICS OF INSTRUCTIONAL OBJECTIVES

A behavioral objective, a performance objective, and an instructional learning outcome all state a consequence of learning. Depending upon the author, these terms are reasonably interchangeable when describing the results of instruction. When goals are written as instructional statements, they specify an observable behavior that the student will demonstrate. According to Mager (1962), instructionally defined objectives have the following characteristics:

1. Objectives graphically describe the terminal behavior – that is, where the student will stand or what he will be doing at the time he has achieved the objective.
2. Objectives include any qualifying conditions or restrictions that must exist for the terminal behavior to be acceptable.
3. Objectives state the criteria of an acceptable performance: time limits, productivity levels, quality control standards, minimum essentials, thresholds, and cutoff scores.

It is important when writing instructional objectives that words are carefully chosen. It is desirable, particularly, to select verbs that are open to fewer interpretations rather than many interpretations. Mager (1975) has illustrated this difference:

Verbs open to many interpretations	*Verbs open to few interpretations*
• to know	• to write
• to understand	• to recite
• to really understand	• to identify
• to fully appreciate	• to differentiate
• to grasp the significance of	• to solve
• to enjoy	• to contrast
• to believe	• to construct
• to trust	• to list
	• to compare

Since many educational goals are too general to be evaluated, specific statements for behavioral outcomes are necessary. Vague statements need to be rephrased in concrete form so that they are measurable. For example, Isaac and Michael (1977) suggest:

Vague: "To improve the self-concept of every child."
Concrete: "To increase the number of positive self-references of a given child in weekly counseling sessons in a six-week period, based on evaluation of authorized tape recordings."

Vague: "To provide the student with a solid foundation in the fundamentals of beginning algebra."
Concrete: "By the end of the unit, the student will be able to solve nine out of ten simple linear equations of the form $2x + 5 = 13$."

Vague: "To provide the first-grade child with an adequate background of reading."
Concrete: "Following the first-grade reading program, the child will be able to read orally a page from a standard first-grade reader, selected by a committee of first-grade teachers, with no more than one error. He/she will also be able to answer correctly two comprehension questions on its content prepared by the same committee."

Vague: "To meet the psychological needs of youth in a changing world."
Concrete: "To conduct a needs assessment at Central High School, using questionnaires and follow-up interviews prepared by a faculty-student committee; to establish a priority of the needs identified; to develop instructional objectives associated with these needs; and to devise procedures and bring about conditions to attain these objectives."

These examples illustrate the need for precise language in instructional objectives. Whereas broad, universal, and "unmeasurable" terminology is acceptable in goal statements, objectives must be specific.

SUMMARY

This chapter introduced instructional objectives: their history, their advantages and disadvantages, and how to construct them.

FOLLOW-UP ACTIVITIES

1. Discuss pros and cons of instructional objectives.
2. Write a paragraph explaining the role of instructional objectives in our approach to curriculum design.
3. Prepare five objectives for a graduate course in curriculum design.
4. Prepare five instructional objectives for your own model curriculum.

REFERENCES

Bobbitt, F. *The Curriculum*. Boston: Houghton Mifflin, 1918.

Bushnell, D. S. "A Systems Approach to Curriculum Change in Secondary Education." *Education Technology*, 10 (May 1970): 46–48.

Charters, W. W. *Curriculum Construction*. New York: Macmillan, 1927.

Cyrs, Jr., T. E. & Lowenthal, R. "A Model for Curriculum Design Using a Systems Aproach." *Audiovisual Instructor*, 15 (January 1970): 16–18.

Gagne, R. M., & Briggs, L. J. *Principles of Instructional Design*. New York: Holt, Rinehart & Winston, 1974.

Gronland, N. *Stating Behavioral Objectives for Classroom Instruction*. 2d. ed. London: Macmillan, 1978.

Isaac, S. & Michael, W. *Handbook in Research and Evaluation*. San Diego: EdITS Publishers, 1977.

Mager, R. *Preparing Instructional Objectives*. Palo Alto, Calif.: Fearon Publishers, 1962.

_____. *Preparing Instructional Objectives*. 2d ed. Palo Alto, Calif.: Fearon Publishers, 1975.

Shane, H. & Weaver, R. *Curriculum Planning for a Society in Transition*. Unpublished manuscript, 1980.

Snedden, D. *Sociological Determination of Objectives in Education*. Philadelphia: J. B. Lippincott, 1921.

Tyler, R. *Basic Principles of Curriculum and Instruction*. Chicago: The University of Chicago Press, 1949.

CHAPTER 6

TURNING GOALS
INTO OBJECTIVES

There is never time to do it right, but always time to do it over.

Meskimen's Law

Education in the United States as well as in other countries around the world has been criticized for relying too heavily on simple objectives that emphasize recall of knowledge. Mastery learning, which is philosophically based on "prior appropriate and current conditions of learning," led to the development of a hierarchy of learning, that is, placing objectives into an order, from simple to most complex, which comprises domains of learning. These domains or classification schemes were developed to aid educators in varying both the types of objectives they write and the difficulty level of these objectives.

Almost three decades ago, Benjamin Bloom and his associates (Bloom, et al. 1956) viewed education as deficient in four major areas: 1) education only meets the needs of the minority of students, 2) a low-level proficiency is all that is achieved, 3) students respond to the expectations presented to them and these are often not appropriate and, 4) academic failure is cumulative. To meet these weaknesses, Bloom conceptualized the domains of learning and, along with other proponents of mastery learning, argued that teaching without use of taxonomies of educational objectives is rigid. They contended that the use of objectives in a hierarchy, beginning at the beginning and going sequentially upward, will significantly improve the educational process. They have research to prove it!

COGNITIVE DOMAIN

The first domain to be developed was the cognitive domain, an area of curriculum concerned with the classification of intellectual behavior. The continuum of cognitive behavior begins with a simple remembering and becomes increasingly complex until the highest order, the process of making judgments, is reached. Bloom and his associates identified a scheme of six basic categories of thinking:

1. *Knowledge* is the lowest level of mental behavior, involving the recognition and recall of facts.
2. *Comprehension* is an understanding of the facts the student has learned.
3. *Application* is the level where a student can use the knowledge acquired to restructure a problem.
4. *Analysis* is the ability to break learning down into its component parts in order to understand the relationships of the parts to one another and to the whole.
5. *Synthesis* is a process whereby the student brings together knowledge possessed in new ways to create new outcomes.
6. *Evaluation* is the highest level of thinking and implies that the learner can think logically about an issue in regard to specific reference points.

Bloom's *cognitive taxonomy* helps curriculum developers examine learning behaviors in terms of their intellectual levels. As used in the implementation process, the classification hierarchy of objectives provides the curriculum designer with a framework for writing objectives which tests the limits of the thinking process. The levels of the domain need not be applied sequentially, although all levels rely upon knowledge. By writing objectives in each level of the cognitive domain, curriculum project teams can provide a greater balance among activities designed to produce cognitive gains. Instruction can also be individualized. See Appendix B for the taxonomy classification of the cognitive domain and for examples.

AFFECTIVE DOMAIN

Just as Bloom and his associates developed the cognitive domain as a hierarchy for intellectual objectives, Krathwohl, Bloom, & Masia (1956) focused upon values and emotions as outcomes or products of instruction. Their book presents a classification system for value responses. The affective domain emphasizes the interests, values, and appreciations of the individual. The continuum begins with the simple behaviors of receiving and responding, and continues through the complex process of characterization. As in the cognitive domain, the levels of behavior appear in a hierarchical scheme:

1. *Receiving* is being aware or conscious of an event.
2. *Responding* is reaction to an event.
3. *Valuing* involves internalizing a belief.
4. *Organization* involves commitment to a set of values.
5. *Characterization* involves total behavior consistent with internalized value systems.

In the affective domain, each step in the hierarchy requires the addition of more commitment or action. For instance, a person who views "the values of differing ethnic groups as acceptable on the basis of a given situation" or "relies on objective approaches to examining contradictory evidence" could be described behaviorally as having moved from low order to high order values (Shane & Weaver 1980).

Affective behavior does not occur without cognition. Every affective behavior, according to Krathwohl, Bloom & Masia (1956), has a cognitive behavior counterpart of some kind. For example, the subcategory 2.1, *Acquiescence in responding,* an objective such as "Willingness to comply with school rules," requires a prior cognitive behavior. Comprehension of these rules and the application of them to daily situations precedes the affective behavior.

In the subcategory 2.2, *Willingness to respond,* students who voluntarily write poems outside of school illustrate how motivation or valuing the writing of poetry may lead to achievement. See Appendix B for taxonomy classification of the affective domain and for examples.

PSYCHOMOTOR DOMAIN

Physical movement behavior has not been studied in educational research nearly as much as activities within the cognitive and affective domains. Many educators have regarded the development of motor skills as the concern of only the physical education department or the dance department. Anita Harrow has produced *A Taxonomy of the Psychomotor Domain* (1972) to furnish curriculum planners with a method for selecting and organizing movement-related activities. Like the preceding classification schemes, motor skills are listed from lower to higher order behaviors. The taxonomy begins with simple behaviors, such as reflex movements, and then catalogs progressively more difficult behaviors, ending with highly skilled movements. This domain is wide-ranging, encompassing all manipulative skills found in sports as well as performing arts such as dance. Similar to the preceding domains, the psychomotor domain is interrelated with the cognitive and affective classifications of behavior. The task of evaluating the content of work relies upon the cognitive aspects of behavior, while analysis of the configurations of the letters emphasizes psychomotor behavior. See Appendix B for taxonomy classification of the psychomotor domain.

WRITING OBJECTIVES

After a thorough examination of the role of instructional objectives in the learning process from goal setting through the use of taxonomies, the team members are ready to translate the goals they prepared in the last phase of their work into objectives. Our format, based on the "Audience, Behavior, Conditions, and Degree" Model developed for the Instructional Development Institute at the University of Southern California, stresses four parts: audience, behavior, conditions, and degree.

Audience.   The audience is defined as a learner, a learner of a particular grade level, or a more specific "learner type." Audience ideally takes into account age levels, grade levels, entering behaviors, learning styles, and other relevant aptitude variables.

Behavior.   The behavior which best illustrates the stated goal is specified from one of the taxonomies — cognitive, affective, or psychomotor. Working with a reference guide to each taxonomy, the behaviors are selected to determine how each goal can be reached. It is often necessary to prepare several behavior statements of the achievement of one goal.

Conditions.   The usual conditions portion of the instructional objective actually includes two parts: the conditions pertaining to the stimulus as well as conditions pertaining to the response. In developing a new curriculum, the "conditions-stimulus" is useful in prescribing exactly what media is required. Whether the material is presented to the learner in paper and pencil format, in a filmstrip, or in a book is an issue that must be clarified at this point. The "conditions-response" prescribes the form of the learner's response. Will it be written, on a worksheet, spoken verbally in a class discussion, or demonstrated through playing a game? Again, the precise statement of the response conditions is useful for future materials of the response as well as any time constraints.

Degree.   This last part of the objective specifies how good the learner's performance must be. Does it need to be 100 percent mastery? Or can it be at the 75 percent level? This decision is made by the curriculum developer, requiring him to state the level of acceptable outcome.

The question of degree requires a justification which may depend upon a number of variables. Issues such as entry level of the learner, state requirements, or health and safety might need to be considered. For example, in a junior high school industrial arts class, 100 percent mastery of the rules regarding use of dangerous machinery is imperative for all learners. In contrast, a competency-based curriculum in art appreciation at the university level might justify a degree of 75 percent completion of four museum-visit assignments as adequate.

A fully written objective format looks like this:

1. The learner (defined according to age, grade, entering behavior, aptitude, etc.).
2. will _____ (verb selected from one of the six levels of Bloom's cognitive taxonomy or from one of the five levels of Krathwohl's affective domain or from one of Harrow's six levels of the psychomotor domain)
3. when presented with _____ (stimulus material), by responding in/on _____ (form of response)
4. such that he masters _____ percent of the behavior.

Two examples of properly written objectives are:

1. At the completion of the six-week instructional unit, all of the students in the special bilingual-bicultural unit will be able to correctly name, in Spanish, twenty of the twenty-five fruits and vegetables. Each student will respond individually to the teacher who will note correct/incorrect responses.
2. Eighty percent of the parents of Head Start children will visit their child's classroom at least twice each month as evidenced by the visitor's sign-up sheet available in the classroom.

In preparing for the writing of the objectives, the list of goals is reviewed. Is the list complete? Does it adequately reflect the selection of content? When the group is satisfied with the goals, the members are ready to begin writing instructional objectives. In executing this task, the team can be divided into dyads (groups of two) or into larger teams (as many as four members). Then each team addresses one goal at a time, developing as many instructional objectives as necessary to achieve that goal. The result will be a series of behaviors, building upon earlier competencies.

All objectives are labeled in sequence, with a letter used for each goal. If goals have been keyed by letters, as recommended earlier, then objectives are tied to them through whole numbers; for example, an objective might be coded A4, the fourth objective toward goal A. This coding is useful for labels at this stage and later in the lesson development phase as well. The form "Instructional Objectives" (See Figure 6.1) can be adapted to the writing process, for it

FIGURE 6.1
Instructional Objectives

PROJECT _____ MODULE OR GRADE _____

We will be writing with the ABCD objective format. Please number objectives with whole numbers (2.0, etc.) and precode them by goals (A, B, F, etc.)

A = Audience   (Who is this for? Who is the learner?)

B = Behavior   (What is he supposed to learn? What is he supposed to be able to do?)

C = Conditions   (With what kind of stimulus—prompts, tools, etc.?)
(In what type of response form—written test, verbal discussion?)

D = Degree   (How well, e.g. 80/80 means 80% of learners master 80% of objective)

Goal _____

Objective _____

A_____

B_____

C_____

D _____

Goal _____

Objective _____

A_____

B_____

C_____

D _____

Goal _____

Objective _____

A_____

B_____

C_____

D _____

FIGURE 6.2
Checklist for Evaluating Objectives

SPECIFIC OBJECTIVES

DEFINITION: An objective is a devised accomplishment which can be verified within a given time and under specifiable conditions which, if attained, advances the student toward a corresponding goal. Each objective should be stated:

a.   So that it specifies learning outcomes which are clearly related to the goal they describe.

b.   So that it specifies only one learning outcome rather than a combination of several outcomes.

c.   In terms of student performance rather than teacher performance.

d.   As a learning product rather than a learning process.

e.   So that it specifies the minimal level of performance which will indicate achievement of the objective.

		Yes	No
1.	Is each specific objective clearly related to the goal it describes?	___	___
2.	Does each specific objective include only one learning outcome?	___	___
3.	Is each specific objective stated in terms of student performance, not teacher performance?	___	___
4.	Is each specific objective stated as a learning product, not process?	___	___
5.	Does each specific objective state the conditions under which the student is to exhibit the desired learning outcome?	___	___
6.	Is the minimal level of performance specified which will indicate achievement of the objective?	___	___

COMMENTS:

From Norman E. Gronlund, *Stating Behavioral Objectives for Classroom Instruction* (London, 1970).

FIGURE 6.3
Evaluating Objectives

Performance objectives developed for program use should be appraised to determine their adequacy and whether they communicate the instructional intent. This may be accomplished by applying the criteria found in the following checklist to each of your program objectives. In this way, errors detected in objectives may be corrected prior to their implementation.

CHECKLIST

		Yes	No
1.	Is each objective stated in measureable terms?		
2.	Does each objective include the six (depending upon format) components necessary to communicate intended outcomes?		
3.	Are the objectives attainable?		
4.	Are the objectives in keeping with the philosophy of the school?		
5.	Is each instructional objective stated in terms of students' terminal behavior rather than subject matter to be covered?		
6.	Is each instructional objective stated in terms of student performance rather than teacher performance?		
7.	Does each instructional objective include only one learning outcome?		
8.	Is each instructional objective stated so that it is relatively independent from other objectives?		

From John Plakos, Marie Plakos, & Robert W. Babcock, *Developing Useful Objectives*. California Evaluation Improvement Project, San Mateo County Improvement Center, 1976.

enables rapid organization of the parts of the objective as they are keyed to the appropriate goal.

Writing teams assume responsibility for a fair share of the objectives. Since the exact number of objectives needed is not known at the outset, the leader may decide with the group simply to divide the list of goals evenly among writing teams. At the beginning of each session, a quota can be established so that groups can depend upon each other. If desired, a group can agree to a simple contract, i.e., "Our group will write objectives for goals A and B within the next two working sessions."

At the end of each session, *before* all of the objectives are written, each group has an opportunity to share its products with the other writing teams. This is important for honest feedback and evaluation. Presenting the writing team's output to the whole group helps to preserve the accountability of each, while at the same time providing opportunity for each team member to act as a critical appraiser. This is the time for suggestions and supportive guidance from other team members.

Checklists for evaluating objectives are useful either at these formative evaluative discussions or when all objectives from all groups
are finished. Two are included here: Gronlund's Checklist for
Evaluating Objectives (See Figure 6.2) and Plakos' Evaluating Objectives (See Figure 6.3). Either one is recommended.

If feedback indicates that more work is needed, then the objectives in question can be returned to the writing team with precise
prescriptions. If more training is needed, it can be arranged at this
point. The process is then repeated back at the "drawing boards," and
the resulting objectives are again brought to the group for evaluation.
When the group has approved all objectives, this step in the process
of curriculum design is complete.

ORGANIZING INSTRUCTIONAL OBJECTIVES
IN ORDER OF IMPORTANCE

After the team has written and evaluated their instructional objectives, their task is to decide which objectives take priority over others.
Some (Popham 1981) state that as few as four or five course objectives are adequate; others advocate more extensive lists of objectives
(Oliva 1982). The decision of how many objectives are necessary,
like the issue of degree of mastery, is reserved for the curriculum
team. Again, the number of objectives used relates to agreed-upon
philosophy of the team.

AN EXAMPLE OF INSTRUCTIONAL OBJECTIVES
AS AN INTEGRAL PART OF CURRICULUM

The example below shows Boblick's (1971) ranked objectives for a
student's writing chemical formulas in a high school chemistry program. (See Figure 6.4). Since no degree statement or "percentage correct" is included in any of the objectives, it is assumed that 100 percent mastery is intended for each behavior.

SUMMARY

The complexity of objectives was described in terms of the taxonomies of learning. This chapter discussed the process of using instructional objectives as a bridge between goals and learning activities
with practical suggestions and forms for team members to use in
work groups and in evaluative procedures. An example of objectives
from a high school chemistry program was included.

FIGURE 6.4
Goal: Writing Chemical Formulas

OBJECTIVES: At the end of this lesson, using paper and pencil materials, the student will be able to:

1. Given the formula of a compound state the chemical name of the compound.
   a. Given a chemical formula of a compound and a list of names and the symbols of the chemical elements, identify those elements present in the compound from the symbols used in the formula.
   b. Given a chemical formula of a compound and a list of names and the formulas of the common radicals, identify those radicals present within the compound.

2. Given the name of a chemical compound, write the formula of that compound.

3. Write the lowest set of integers which gives a net oxidation number of zero for the compound as subscripts following the appropriate symbol or radical.

4. Select a set of integers which, when multiplied by the number of moles of each element and/or radical within the formula, will give a net oxidation number of zero.

5. Interpret a sum of zero for the oxidation numbers of the elements within a formula as an indication that the formula is correctly written.

6. Calculate the sum of the oxidation numbers of the elements comprising the compound.

7. Calculate the number of moles of each element that comprise a radical within a compound by multiplying the number of moles of each element within the radical by the subscript following the parentheses which enclose the radical.

8. Indicate the presence of two or more moles of a radical within one mole of the compound by enclosing the formula of the radical in parentheses and placing outside and following the parentheses the subscript which numerically equals the number of moles of the radical present.

9. Interpret the subscript following a chemical symbol or radical within a formula as indicating the number of moles of that element or radical within one mole of the compound.

10. Write the element or radical with the most positive oxidation number first (leftmost) in the formula.

11. Write the element or radical with the most negative oxidation number last (rightmost) in the formula.

12. Define a chemical radical.

13. Define a formula as representing one mole of a chemical compound.

FOLLOW-UP ACTIVITIES

1. Give an example of an objective from the cognitive domain.
2. Give an example of an objective from the affective domain.
3 . Give an example of an objective from the psychomotor domain.
4. Write an objective using the "ABCD" format from the cognitive, affective, and psychomotor domain.
5. Evaluate the objectives for your project using either Gronlund's or Plakos's checklist.

6. Devise a plan for dividing the task of writing objectives from goals so that the work is shared equally by all project team members.
7. Explain how quality of objectives is controlled in this approach.
8. Explain why it is important to specify "conditions" so carefully.

REFERENCES

Bloom, B. S; Engelhart, M. D.; Furst, E. J.; Hill, W. K.; & Krathwohl, D. R. *Taxonomy of Educational Objectives. Handbook I: Cognitive Domain.* New York: David McKay, 1956.

Boblick, J. M. "Applying the Systems-Approach to Curriculum Development in the Science Classroom." *Science Education* 55 (1971): 103–13.

Gagne, R. M. & Briggs, L. J. *Principles of Instructional Design.* New York: Holt, Rinehart, & Winston, 1974.

Gronlund, N. E. *Stating Behavioral Objectives for Classroom Instruction.* London: Macmillan, 1970.

Harrow, A. *A Taxonomy of the Psychomotor Domain.* New York: David McKay, 1972.

Isaac, S. & Michael, W. *Handbook in Research and Evaluation.* San Diego: EdITS Publishers, 1977.

Krathwohl, D. R.; Bloom, B. S.; & Masia, B. B. *Taxonomy of Educational Objectives, Handbook II: Affective Domain.* New York: David McKay, 1956.

Mager, R. *Preparing Instructional Objectives.* 2d ed. Palo Alto, Calif.: Fearon Publishers, 1975.

Metfessel, N. S.; Michael, W. B.; & Kirsner, D. A. "Instruction of Bloom's and Kratwohl's Taxonomies for the Writing of Educational Objectives." *Psychology in the Schools* 6 (July 1969): 227–31.

Oliva, Peter F. *Developing Curriculum.* Boston: Little Brown, 1982.

Plakos, J.; Plakos, M. E.; & Babcock, R. W. *Developing Useful Objectives.* California Evaluation Improvement Project, San Mateo County Evaluation Improvement Center, 1976.

Popham, J. *Modern Educational Measurement.* Englewood Cliffs, New Jersey: Prentice-Hall, 1981.

Shane, H., & Weaver, R. *Curriculum Design for a Society in Transition.* Unpublished manuscript, 1980.

CHAPTER 7

GENERATING APPROPRIATE LESSONS

For want of a nail, the shoe was lost.

George Herbert

"To test is not to teach" was the assertion of Dr. Gordon Cawelti at the Sixth Annual Conference and Exhibition on Measurement and Evaluation in Pasadena, California. Cawelti, Executive Director of the Association for Supervision and Curriculum Development, pointed to an over-concern with instructional objectives in the past few years; proper statements of objectives had, unfortunately, become the singular goal of curriculum design. We must, Cawelti insisted, move *beyond* instructional objectives (Cawelti 1979).

Of course, objectives are critical, but emphasis in the 1980s needs to be upon the selection of content and upon organization of learning experiences. With well-written instructional objectives in hand, curriculum development must address issues of teaching materials and lesson plans.

Too often in the past objectives were prepared according to correct criteria, and then the curriculum development process broke down. Teachers were left with long lists of objectives but with no ideas on how they could help their students achieve them. Some persons might be impressed by well-stated objectives standing alone, but teachers in their classroom judge the quality of the curriculum by its model lessons.

Building upon the objectives written by the project team during the previous phase, the task in this chapter is to create lessons that will facilitate the students' achievement of those objectives (See Figure 7.1). The group will look at criteria for lesson development. It is the group's decision to work within units of study or within sequen-

FIGURE 7.1
Generate Appropriate Lessons

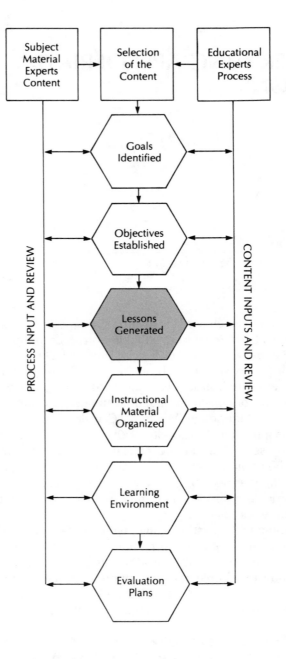

tial individual lessons. Group members must also agree upon a suitable format. They must decide upon their subteam responsibilities, and ultimately they must decide the scope and sequence of the lessons.

WHAT THE TEAM NEEDS TO KNOW ABOUT CREATING LESSONS

Before the team begins to write the first lesson, each member begins with a special advantage: professional teaching experience. Each has some genuine insight into what kinds of lesson activities learners really can relate to—and about what activities will not be meaningful, which is equally valuable. Each participant knows something about the target learners. Furthermore, since all team members have participated in the stating of goals and objectives, they all know where the learner needs to go. At this point we must recall our Cheshire Cat experience and be reminded that *any* path will *not* do. The purpose now is to choose the *best* path to the achievement of the stated instructional objectives.

Some background of the theoretical work on developing curriculum is helpful here. The hard question is: "With all the possible lessons one could prepare for any objective outcome, how does one decide on which lesson to include?" A brief review of the works of Taba (1962), McNeil (1981), and Bloom et al. (1956) offers some ideas which will help a teacher decide what to choose.

ESTABLISHING CRITERIA FOR LESSON PLANNING

How do curriculum development teams make decisions regarding content, organization, and learning experiences? Taba's (1962) three general questions suggest the rationale which guides the conception of an objectives model of curriculum design:

1. What are the demands and the requirements of the culture in which the curriculum will operate?
2. What do we know about the learning process and the nature of the learner?
3. What is the nature of knowledge? What are the characteristics and contributions of the disciplines?

In other words, the rationale for any objective model for curriculum design is that curricula originate from the demands and requirements of the society, that curricula be firmly grounded in our knowledge of the learner and the learning process, and that curricula reflect an understanding of the nature of knowledge.

Another view of selecting learning activities focuses on McNeil's

(1981) five kinds of criteria for guiding and justifying the selection of learning activities: philosophical, psychological, technological, political, and practical.

Philosophical Criteria

In philosophical considerations of curriculum content, values are the chief basis for judging proposed learning activities. These value positions are evident in the following curriculum-makers' dilemmas:

1. Learning activities should be immediately enjoyable but also lead to desirable future experiences. The teacher decides which side of this issue is more important to the lesson and to overall goals.
2. Learning activities should show the ideal: the just, the beautiful, and the honorable. Learning activities should also show life as it is, including corruption, violence, and the profane. The materials chosen by the teacher reflect his or her values; an English teacher introducing poetry to students could choose the romantic poetry of Lord Byron or the realistic poetry of Theodore Roethke, thereby suggesting values or beliefs about life.
3. Learning activities can deal with the thinking, feeling, and acting of the group to which the learner belongs; or deal with he thinking, feeling, and acting of groups other than those to which the learner belongs. This dilemma has been the focus of multicultural education and the social sciences.
4. Learning activities should minimize human variability by stressing common outlooks and capacities, but it should also increase variability by stressing individuality. This dilemma is basically a day-to-day stress on the teacher who works with a group of students, while at the same time meeting the individual needs of the learners. The decision of what is most important, the group or the individual need, is entirely up to the teacher, again reflecting the teacher's values.
5. Whether the teacher stresses cooperation so that individuals share in achieving a common goal, or stresses competition so that an able student may excel as an individual, is the teacher's choice. What is accomplished in the classroom will be affected by this basic decision.
6. Whereas some teachers allow students to clarify their own positions on moral and controversial issues, other teachers instruct their students in the values of moral and intellectual integrity. Although there are variations on this conflict, with very few teachers dogmatically adhering to one side or the other, the resolution of the dilemma affects the way students learn and how they learn.

Psychological Criteria

Psychological beliefs regarding learning can also determine how a learning activity is presented. A teacher who has a closed view of learning would feel that learning activities should:

1. Be under the direct influence of the teacher who demonstrates in order that the learner will imitate and acquire knowledge.
2. Be pleasant and comfortable for the student.
3. Teach one thing at a time but teach it to mastery, simplify the environment, and give enough instances to help the learner abstract desired generalizations.
4. Allow the learner to acquire simple basic patterns before exposure to higher orders of learning.
5. Allow the learner to see and imitate great models of speaking, feeling, and acting.
6. Feature repetitive practice on a skill not mastered.

A teacher with an opened-minded approach to learning would project psychological beliefs that learning activities should:

1. Be removed from direct teacher influence, allowing self actualization by finding meaning in a situation where the teacher is a resource person.
2. Allow for hardship and perplexity, so that significant growth can take place.
3. Bring about several outcomes at once, helping students develop interests and attitudes as well as cognitive growth.
4. Allow the learner to grasp the meaning and organization of the whole before proceeding to study the parts.
5. Allow the learner to create and practice new and different ways of talking, feeling, and acting.
6. Feature novel and varied approaches to an unlearned skill.

Teachers' psychological beliefs are rarely extremely open-minded or closed-minded in every subject area they teach. However, it is important to keep these distinctions in mind when making up lessons. Teachers who have carefully thought through a philosophy and a psychology of teaching will be able to generate more appropriate lessons.

Technological Criteria

A third set of criteria originates in the work of educational technologists such as Benjamin Bloom. Our book also relies upon the instructional technology tradition:

1. The objectives for the activity are in behavioral terms.
2. A task analysis has been made whereby components of a complex behavior are identified and a relationship between the tasks and the final objectives is specified.
3. Learning activities are directly related to the behavior and content of the specified objectives.
4. Evaluation procedures are comparable to objectives:
   a. There is immediate feedback regarding the adequacy of the learner's responses.
   b. There are criterion-referenced tests that measure achievement toward objectives.
   c. Attention is given to evaluating both the process, by which the learner learns, and the product, or what the learner learns.
5. The product or activity has been carefully field-tested.

Political Criteria

McNeil's fourth set of criteria are political concerns which have resulted in these legal requirements:

1. Teaching materials must portray both men and women in their full range of leadership, occupation, and domestic roles without demeaning, stereotyping, or patronizing references in regard to either sex.
2. Material must portray, without significant omission, the historical role of members of racial, ethnic, and cultural groups, including their contributions and achievements in all areas of life.
3. Materials must portray members of cultural groups without demeaning, stereotyping, or patronizing references concerning their heritage, characteristics, or lifestyle.

Practical Criterion

The final criterion is practicality, particularly in the form of economy. Project members must weigh the cost of providing a certain learning experience. As curriculum developers well know, the new program can be expensive in outright costs of materials, maintenance, supplementary materials, and training.

WHAT ABOUT SCOPE?

Making decisions about *scope* has never been easy. For some curriculum development projects, the term *scope* has been loosely defined as "what the curriculum will include." It has been discussed as the "the breadth" of the content in any course or grade level. Some even say the scope is everything that is in the course of study. More helpful, perhaps, is the notion that scope includes the topics, learning experiences, activities, focal points, and organizing centers of the curriculum.

Many curriculum developers have defined scope in terms of textbooks or even pages in textbooks; the author and publisher were regarded as experts, and their work was accepted as the sum total of the scope of the curriculum. Sometimes, but only rarely we believe, one can find an existing book that encompasses the topics and learning activities necessary for a particular project. Most times, however, it is a much more complicated problem.

In the model we are using, there is a built-in background when we define the scope of our curriculum. Since the conceptual framework, the goals, and the objectives have already been stated, many of the focal points of the curriculum have been identified. We know what we want to emphasize. Lessons can then be built around those organizing centers.

WHAT ABOUT SEQUENCE?

If scope was "the what" of curriculum then *sequence* is "the when" (Oliva 1982). Sequencing the curriculum refers to the best order of presenting the materials, lessons, and activities. There are several successful ways to establish an effective sequence to curriculum.

Oliva offers eight ways of arranging the content: from simple to complex as in programmed instruction, chronological order (a historical approach), reverse chronological order, historical themes, from near to far (in geographical terms), from far to near, from concrete to abstract, from general to specific.

Just as in determining the scope, our model has prepared the team for sequencing. A continuum of behaviors was prepared when objectives were written.

CONTINUUM OF BEHAVIORS

With these criteria for lesson planning, scope, and sequence in mind, and fully aware that they are in another position to expand their roles as decision makers, the project team members address the task of generating lessons from objectives. The objectives as they now stand can become a continuum of behaviors, which is simply a list of student outcomes in order of difficulty or in the order the student can achieve them most readily.

How do we establish such a continuum? The important question is, "What does the student need to know first?" An example of a set of behaviors is taken from the critical thinking curriculum (Los Angeles City Schools, 1975): "Cognitive Objectives Leading to Proficiency in Judging Whether a Statement Follows from the Premise" (See Figure

FIGURE 7.2
Cognitive Objectives Leading to Proficiency in Judging Whether a Statement
Follows from the Premise

ENTRY
BEHAVIOR

I.   The learner will visualize and/or auralize the total story,
     speech, or activity.

II. The learner will identify the topic sentences, main thought,
     or conclusion.

III. The learner will discriminate and select relevant statements.

IV. The learner will restate or reorder relevant information in an
     understandable, clear format.

V.   The learner will state a premise (it may be right or wrong).

VI. The learner will recognize that signal words (context clues)
     can imply there is a premise (i.e., for, since, because, all,
     some, none, not, if-then, or, unless, etc.).

VII. The learner will recognize that a statement which classifies
     can imply there is a premise.

VIII. The learner will isolate the premise.

IX. The learner will reflect on the above processes and recognize
     there was a line of reasoning.

TERMINAL
BEHAVIOR

7.2). Clearly, a number of objectives are likely to be achieved in one
lesson. The problem for the project team is how to classify the objectives in an orderly manner.

OBJECTIVES MATRIX

In our approach the team begins with an advantage at this point in
the process. In the first place, every objective has a code letter or
number which can be traced back through the objective to the goal.
Each objective also has been assigned a sequential number which
was derived from the goal. An objective matrix, which indicates goal
origin and different grade levels of objectives, is shown in Figure 7.3.

Grade-level designations are placed across the top of the matrix.
In this matrix grades K–6 are displayed. Goal letters are placed in a
vertical column on the left-hand side of the matrix, showing goals in
their categories. The assignment of writing specific objectives to
match goals is clarified in this process. For example, if a group were
to work on the goal "C_1," they could work first on an objective for the
kindergarten, "C_{K1}," and then on "C_{11}" and then "C_{21}", continuing this
process until all objectives had been considered.

This kind of matrix is useful as a checklist when the writing is

FIGURE 7.3
Objectives Matrix for Solar Energy Project

Goal \ Grade	K	1	2	3	4	5	6
Z_1	Z_{K1}	Z_{11}	Z_{21}	Z_{31}	Z_{41}	Z_{51}	Z_{61}
A_1	A_{K1}	A_{11}	A_{21}	A_{31}	A_{41}	A_{51}	A_{61}
A_2	A_{K2}	A_{12}	A_{22}	A_{32}	A_{42}	·	·
A_3	A_{K3}	A_{13}	·	·	·	·	·
A_4	A_{K4}	A_{14}	·	·	·	·	·
B_1	B_{K1}	B_{11}	B_{21}	B_{31}	B_{41}	B_{51}	
B_2	B_{K2}	B_{12}	B_{22}	B_{32}	B_{42}	B_{52}	
B_3	B_{K3}	B_{13}					
B_4	B_{K4}	B_{14}					
B_5	B_{K5}	B_{15}					
B_6	B_{K6}	B_{16}					
B_7	B_{K7}	B_{17}					
B_8	B_{K8}	B_{18}					
C_1	C_{K1}	C_{11}					
D_1	D_{K2}	D_{11}					
D_2	D_{K2}	D					
G_1	G_{K1}						

Z_{ij}
A_{ij}
B_{ij} } ith Grade
C_{ij}
D_{ij}
G_{ij} } jth Objective or Goal

finished, to make sure that objectives have been produced for every goal at every level. This process is appropriate and useful if the curriculum calls for a variety of lessons at a number of levels. The example shown in Figure 7.4 is a model lesson on critical thinking for Los Angeles City Schools for children at various levels of cognitive development in the primary grades. Figure 7.5 is another example of lessons toward the same continuum objectives, which aimed at learners at the middle grade level.

TASK ANALYSIS

One important characteristic of the sequence of behaviors in the critical thinking lessons is that each new behavior is based on those preceding it. A task analysis was used in compiling these lessons. An explanation on how the student bridges the gap between entry behaviors and terminal behaviors is contained in the following paragraphs.

A task analysis may be represented as a hierarchy of entering behaviors, terminal objectives, and intermediate objectives. It is a list of tasks from the simplest to the most complex. Whereas *entering behaviors* are those behaviors that must already exist in a learner's repertoire to begin a learning sequence, *enabling or intermediate objectives* are those which must be achieved in the step-by-step progression toward the final outcome, the *terminal behavior*. An example of an enabling objective within the high school science package

FIGURE 7.4
Model Lesson for Primary Grades

A CRITICAL THINKER IS CHARACTERIZED BY PROFICIENCY IN
JUDGING WHETHER A STATEMENT FOLLOWS A PREMISE

OBJECTIVES

1. The learner recognizes that a premise is "a given" (a declarative
   sentence/sentences).
2. The learner identifies the premise.
   Some premises are explicit (stated) – e.g., My premise is

   _____.

   Some premises are implicit (not stated but assumed).
3. The learner recognizes that the statement which follows from
   the premise reflects a logical/sequential line of reasoning.

PERFORMANCE OBJECTIVE

Given a set of blocks of various shapes, sizes, and colors, the
learner will discover, discriminate, select, identify, and isolate a
"given" premise. The premise is that only brown squares (any size,
any thickness) may be buildings in "My City."

MATERIALS:

Six feet (6') of string
Blocks of various colors, shapes, and sizes

CLASSROOM ORGANIZATION:

The learners will be grouped so that all the children can see "My City."
"My City" is a circle made with the six feet of string.

PROCEDURE:

THE LEARNER WILL VISUALIZE AND/OR AURALIZE THE TOTAL
STORY, SPEECH, OR ACTIVITY.

1. The teacher defines the rules of the game.

1. "I'm building a city and you may add buildings to My City. Buildings of a certain size, shape, and color may be built in My City. Can you discover what kind of buildings will be built in My City?"

THE LEARNER WILL IDENTIFY THE TOPIC SENTENCES, MAIN
THOUGHT, OR CONCLUSION.

2. The teacher encourages each learner to see if a block may belong to "My City."

2. "Look at your block(s)! Do you think it(they) belongs(belong) in My City?"

THE LEARNER WILL DISCRIMINATE AND SELECT RELEVANT
STATEMENTS.

THE LEARNER WILL RESTATE OR REORDER RELEVANT INFOR-
MATION IN AN UNDERSTANDABLE, CLEAR FORMAT.

3. The teacher encourages each child to try his or her block to see if it belongs in "My City."

3. If the block belongs in "My City," "Yes, this building belongs in My City." If not, "No, this building does not belong in My City."

> THE LEARNER WILL STATE A PREMISE (IT MAY BE RIGHT OR WRONG).

4. The teacher recognizes that the child has tentatively identified the premise.

4. "What kind of buildings are in My City?"

> THE LEARNER WILL RECOGNIZE THAT SIGNAL WORDS (CONTEXT CLUES) CAN IMPLY THERE IS A PREMISE (i.e., FOR, SINCE, BECAUSE, ALL, SOME, NONE, NOT, IF-THEN, OR, UNLESS, etc.).

> THE LEARNER WILL RECOGNIZE THAT A STATEMENT WHICH CLASSIFIES CAN IMPLY THERE IS A PREMISE.

5. The teacher encouarges the children to test the premise.

5. The learner's identification is that brown blocks belong in "My City." "If you have a brown block, let's see if it belongs in My City."

As various brown blocks are tried and accepted or rejected, the teacher will help the children to identify the reasoning process.

> THE LEARNER WILL ISOLATE THE PREMISE.

> THE LEARNER WILL REFLECT ON THE ABOVE PROCESSES AND RECOGNIZE THAT THERE WAS A LINE OF REASONING.

6. The teacher recognizes that the learner has isolated the "given" premise.

EXTENDED ACTIVITIES:

1. Repeat the game with other premises.
2. Play the game with two boundaries, using a different premise for each.
3. Play the game with other "buildings" (i.e., short vowels, consonant blends, parts of speech, prime numbers, etc.).
4. Use three boundaries and develop the concept of intersection (set theory).
5. Establish an interest center where children may play the game.
6. The learners develop a premise and create an interest center.

ENRICHMENT ACTIVITIES:

1. Visit or study pictures of a given block of buildings and try to discover the premise for types of buildings.
2. Have an architect visit the class to discuss the different architectural styles related to various historical periods.
3. Take walking trips to discover the number of commercial buildings as opposed to the number of residential buildings.
4. Have city planning commissioners visit the class to discuss the planning of a city.

FIGURE 7.5
Model Lesson for Middle Grade Level

A CRITICAL THINKER IS CHARACTERIZED BY PROFICIENCY IN JUDGING WHETHER A STATEMENT FOLLOWS A PREMISE

OBJECTIVES

1. The learner recognizes that a premise is "a given" (a declarative sentence/sentences).
2. The learner identifies the premise.
   Some premises are explicit (stated) – e.g., My premise is
   _____.
   Some premises are implicit (not stated but assumed).
3. The learner recognizes that the statement which follows from the premise reflects a logical/sequential line of reasoning.

PERFORMANCE OBJECTIVE

Give a list of related words, the learner will discover, discriminate, select, identify, and isolate a "given" premise. The premise is that only words with double consonants are included in the "like" column.

MATERIALS:

Chalkboard
Chalk

CLASSROOM ORGANIZATION:

The learners will be grouped in a functional classroom.

PROCEDURE:

THE LEARNER WILL VISUALIZE AND/OR AURALIZE THE TOTAL STORY, SPEECH, OR ACTIVITY.

---

1. The teacher defines the rules of the game.

1. "My Aunt Fanny came to visit me last night." Write *Aunt Fanny* on the chalkboard. "She's rather odd. She has very particular likes and dislikes." Write *likes* and *doesn't like* as column headings under *Aunt Fanny.*

THE LEARNER WILL IDENTIFY THE TOPIC SENTENCES, MAIN THOUGHT, OR CONCLUSION.

---

2. The teacher encourages each learner to discover the commonality of the words in each list, and the difference between the words of a pair. The title of the game offers the clue.

2. "Aunt Fanny likes apples, but she doesn't like oranges." The teacher writes 'apples' under *likes* and 'oranges' under *doesn't like.* "I'm going to write more pairs of words, and as soon as you know my premise, you may suggest a pair of words. But, *don't tell the rule of the game.*" (Other pairs of words could be any appropriate nouns within a category, e.g., likes lettuce, doesn't like spinach; likes broccoli, doesn't like turnips. *Avoid* using nouns of different classes, e.g., likes apples, doesn't like fruit; or likes lettuce,

doesn't like vegetables. These make it more difficult for the learner to identify the premise.)

> THE LEARNER WILL DISCRIMINATE AND SELECT RELEVANT STATEMENTS.

> THE LEARNER WILL RESTATE OR REORDER RELEVANT INFORMATION IN AN UNDERSTANDABLE, CLEAR FORMAT.

3. The teacher encourages each learner to verbalize a pair of words.

3. The teacher adds more pairs of words to the list. Children suggest pairs of words. Teacher adds to the list any pair that fits the premise.

> THE LEARNER WILL STATE A PREMISE (IT MAY BE RIGHT OR WRONG).

4. The teacher recognizes that the learner has tentatively identified the premise.

4, 5. When a learner indicates that he or she knows the rule, let the student try another pair of words to test his or her premise. If the pair fits the premise, write them in the appropriate column. If they do not fit the premise, say, "No, Aunt Fanny likes (doesn't like) _(word)_," and do not write them.

> THE LEARNERS WILL RECOGNIZE THAT SIGNAL WORDS (CONTEXT CLUES) CAN IMPLY THERE IS A PREMISE (i.e., FOR, SINCE, BECAUSE, ALL, SOME, NONE, NOT, IF-THEN, OR, UNLESS, etc.).

> THE LEARNER WILL RECOGNIZE THAT A STATEMENT WHICH CLASSIFIES CAN IMPLY THERE IS A PREMISE.

5. The teacher encourages the learner to test the premise.

> THE LEARNER WILL ISOLATE THE PREMISE.

> THE LEARNER WILL REFLECT ON THE ABOVE PROCESSES AND RECOGNIZE THAT THERE WAS A LINE OF REASONING.

6. The teacher recognizes that the learner has isolated the "given" premise.

EXTENDED ACTIVITIES:

1. Repeat the game using variations of vowels, letter combinations, capitalization of beginnings and endings, etc.
2. Repeat the game using geometric shapes (e.g., all right angles are correct, anything else is incorrect).
3. Repeat the game using various classifications (e.g., reptiles, fruits, mammals).
4. The learners develop a premise and create an interest center.

is: From observing a plant, the student identifies three possible outcomes when the plant is deprived of light for three weeks.

This task analysis will prove to be extremely helpful in the next step of our model: organizing instructional materials. Again, the feedback function of this method is important. With each new step that the project team completes, from instructional objective writing to task analysis, the members have developed more fully the plan for their lesson.

This fuller emergence of the lesson enables the team to better evaluate progress to date. The feedback loops within the model, as outlined in Chapter 1, provide a means by which the team, on the basis of a current discovery or insight, may return to previously completed steps and revise them in terms of the new information. When constructing a sequence of objectives, in particular, it is common to find that an essential entering behavior has not been stated in the objectives. The feedback loops provide the means by which the team returns to change or add to the original set of objectives.

BEGINNING TO WRITE LESSONS

After analyzing the sequence of objectives in goal *families,* the project team decides how the members would like to work. There are at least two possible methods: Lessons can be prepared for a certain group of learners, designated by the "A" part of each objective across all objectives; or lessons can be prepared based on behaviors to meet certain lettered goals, keyed to particular learner characteristics.

In the case of the solar energy curriculum, in Appendix A, the group chose the second alternative above. In approaching the lesson writing task, the group assured themselves that they had developed a complete matrix with goals reflected in discrete instructional objectives on seven learner levels, in grades K–6. Even though some of the developers objected to the grade-level labels, they were satisfied that, nevertheless, their objectives were on a continuum from entry to terminal behavior. They decided to work on individual lessons rather than whole units at the outset.

APPROPRIATE FORMS

If the group members have the opportunity to choose their own format (and if it was not specified in the given information at the time of their recruitment), they do. The accompanying form (See Figure 7.6) requires the writer to identify the goal and objectives of each lesson, providing space for overview, materials, vocabulary, activities, extension activities, related curriculum, and bibliography and resources. We recommend this form for all lesson plans, but of course other formats are acceptable.

FIGURE 7.6
Lesson Plan Form

Please fill out one of these for each lesson for each grade or level.

Grade _____ Lesson_____ Week _____

1. GOAL(S)

   OBJECTIVE(S)

2. OVERVIEW

3. MATERIALS:
   Please indicate: N for necessary; H for helpful; L for luxury.

4. LESSON PLAN

   A. VOCABULARY:

   B. MATERIALS:

   C. ACTIVITIES:
      (Outline)

      (Description)

   D. EVALUATION:

5. EXTENSION ACTIVITIES:

6. RELATED CURRICULUM:

7. BIBLIOGRAPHY AND RESOURCES:

Figure 7.7, an example of an experimental format, is a model lesson from the critical thinking curriculum, with cognitive and affective objectives included at the end. If neither of these formats is satisfactory to the project team, then members can make their own. They must, however, unanimously agree to use it.

WORKING GROUPS

By this step in the process, the team members are used to working on tasks in small groups and then sharing their products for evaluation with the group at large. The writing of lessons continues this process, again relying upon individual preference and expertise. In the solar energy curriculum, the participants were selected on the basis of their experience with learners of various ages, K–6; therefore, they were pleased to be in working groups assigned to address the learner audience they knew best.

Time limits on lesson writing are important. Team members are

FIGURE 7.7
Model Lesson for Early Primary Grades

A CRITICAL THINKER IS CHARACTERIZED BY PROFICIENCY IN JUDGING WHETHER SOMETHING IS AN ASSUMPTION

GOALS

1. Recognition that an assumption is an explicit or implicit understanding which may have been used in a line of reasoning leading to a conclusion.
2. Recognition that a prediction could not occur if the alleged assumption is false.
3. Recognition that a community of experts in the field would not accept the position, conclusion, or argument without believing the assumption to be true.
4. Recognition that the presupposition must be true for a given statement to make sense.

To the Teacher:

An assumption is an assertion about reality which is unproved or debatable. It is a statement taken for granted. In logic, an assumption specifically designates the minor or second premise in a syllogism (Hayakawa).

A syllogism is an argument or form of reasoning in which two statements or premises are made and a logical conclusion is drawn from them (Webster, *New World Dictionary*).

Understanding an assumption is a basic part of thinking critically. In order to teach this skill meaningfully, the learner and the teacher must work together to combine the learning process and learning outcomes.

An argument refers to discussion in which there is a disagreement and suggests the use of logic and the bringing forth of facts to support or refute a point.

INSTRUCTIONAL OBJECTIVES

1. The learner compares the assumption as understood with personal experience.
2. The learner recognizes an assumption may be used as a premise.
3. The learner searches for an implicit assumption in the line of reasoning.

DEFINITIONS:

Premise: Implies the setting forth of a proposition on which a conclusion can be based plus understanding the meaning of the words.
Implicit: Not directly stated; suggested or to be understood though not plainly expressed.

MATERIALS:

Color slides of bats and birds; opaque projector
Textbook: *Baker's Dozen*, "The Bat on the Farm", pp. 12–14; Birds, p. 80
World Book Encyclopedia, "Birds", pp. 250–255; "Bats", pp. 116–117
Pamphlet: Wildlife Bulletin, "Bats", U.S. Department of the Interior
Note to Teacher: Do not use books until slides are shown and assumption has been made.

PROCEDURE:

The teacher and children look at the color slides of the bats and birds. They discuss the characteristics of both.

Teacher:
"As we looked carefully at the slides of the bats and birds, we saw certain characteristics they both have." (The teacher makes a list of characteristics on the chalkboard.)

The bat . . .
1. has wings.
2. flies at night.
3. hangs upside down
   from rafters.
4. looks like a mouse.
5. has fur.
6. has a backbone.

The bird . . .
1. has wings.
2. has beak or bill.
3. has feathers.
4. has a backbone.
5. has two legs.
6. flies (usually during the day).

Teacher and learners compare likenesses and differences of both animals.

Teacher: "What is a bat?" (Allow children time for discussion of reasons for choices.)

Learner: "Since the bat has wings and can fly, it is a bird."

Teacher: "Which part of this statement do we know to be true?"

Learner: "The first part that says, *since the bat has wings and can fly.*"

Teacher and learners also use opaque projector to study bat and bird pictures.

Teacher defines *characteristics* as the word that tells how animals look and act.

Teacher leads children until someone gives a response that will contain an if, when, since, or but statement.

The learner recognizes that there are certain signal words which indicate assumption making (*since, because, if, and when*).

Teacher: "Now we must find out if the bat is a bird because so far we only are assuming that to be true."

Learner: "How can we find out?"

Second Learner: "We have a barn and I have seen bats flying around. I know they are birds because they fly."

> Teacher defines the word *assuming* as meaning "taken for granted."

> Here the learner compares assumption with personal experience. The assumption is that since birds have wings and fly, the bat must be a bird as it has wings and it can fly.

Third Learner: "We can read in our textbook or check the dictionary and the encyclopedia."

> Here the learner discovers authorities, selects what authorities have to say, and begins to collect data.

Teacher: "Will someone read the information to us? We will listen to see if we can find the answers to our question. Will someone please restate the question?"

Fourth Learner: "Is the bat a bird? Are all animals that fly birds?"

> Here the learner restates the presupposition as a question and isolates the problem or conflict.

> The learner recognizes that the answer must be yes or no.

First Learner reads information obtained from text and other sources:

1. A bat has fur.
2. Some bats sleep in barns. Some sleep in caves and vacant buildings.
3. A bat has sharp teeth and claws.
4. A bat bears its young live.
5. A bat feeds its young milk from its own body. All animals that bear their own young live and feed them milk from their own bodies are called mammals.
6. A bat sends out shrill sharp sounds.

> Learner cites facts and information (obtained from authorities) that are pertinent to the question.

Second Learner reads information gathered about birds:

1. A bird has a beak or a bill.
2. A bird has hollow bones.
3. A bird lays eggs to hatch its young.
4. A bird carries seeds, nuts, berries, to its young.
5. A bird has feathers.
6. A bird has two legs.
7. Some birds can chirp and sing.

Teacher: "Now, with the new facts we have learned, is our first assumption correct?"

Learners: "No."
Teacher: "What now would we say?"
Learners: "We would say a bat is not a bird. A bat is a mammal."

Learner considers new evidence and decides original assumption is wrong.
Learner makes new assumption based on additional facts and authorities, reflects on the process employed, and recognizes use of critical thinking.

A LESSON IN CRITICAL THINKING HAS TWO MAJOR COMPONENTS— AFFECTIVE AND COGNITIVE:

Affective:
The learner assumes responsibility for reading the story and studying the pictures.
The learner voluntarily pursues the appropriate meaning of words.
The learner desires to know the answers to the questions.
The learner voluntarily seeks authorities to prove or disprove the assumptions.
The learner assumes the responsibility of finding creative ways to solve problems.

Cognitive:
The learner recognizes words in context and demonstrates his ability to use them as he explains the assumption.
The learner develops ways to use the words *if, so, when, because, since,* etc.
The learner recognizes cause-and-effect relationships and uses the knowledge to relate parts to a whole.
The learner compares, contrasts, and extends boundaries of topics.
The learner knows how to make discriminating choices.
The learner recognizes and understands the meaning of contrasting statements.
The learner states the assumption in the opposite form.
The learner recognizes a need for a logical conclusion based on evidence.
The learner comes to a conclusion (a bat is not a bird; it is a mammal).

BIBLIOGRAPHY:

Durr, William. *Vistas in Reading.* International Reading Association, 1966.
Dawson, Mildred; Newman, Georgiana. *Language Teaching in Kindergarten and Early Primary Grades.* Harcourt, Brace & World, 1966.
Ennis, Robert. A definition of critical thinking. *Harvard Educational Review.*
Gronlund, Norman E. *Stating Behavioral Objectives for Classroom Instruction,* Macmillan.
Hayakawa, S. A. *A Modern Guide to Synonyms,* Funk & Wagnalls, Inc.
Newman, Georgiana; Dawson, Mildred. *Baker's Dozen.* Field Educational Publications, 1970.
Reader's Digest, *Our Amazing World of Nature.*
Wildlife Pamphlet: "Bats," U.S. Department of the Interior.
World Book Encyclopedia.

encouraged to block out lessons first, using the form approved by the group. They can later go back and expand ideas if necessary. If dialogue is important, as in the critical thinking examples, it must be written to sufficient degree for another teacher to understand and use it. In short, the more complete the lesson, the better—especially since materials will be developed to fit the needs prescribed in each lesson.

SUMMARY

Generating appropriate lessons from objectives was the topic of this chapter. Criteria for what should be included in lessons was outlined, and plans for arranging behavioral objectives into a continuum were stressed. Examples from the critical thinking curriculum were cited as lists of tasks from entry to terminal behavior. An objectives matrix was recommended so that lessons could be planned for different learners at different levels to master the same concept. In writing their own lessons, each project team decides its own content organization, format, working groups, and time limits. Members continue to support and evaluate the products of their colleagues.

FOLLOW-UP ACTIVITIES

1. State one rule for lesson writing.
2. Discuss five criteria for choices in lesson writing.
3. Write one lesson for your project, using the recommended form.
4. Explain why it is useful to develop an objective matrix similar to Figure 7.3.
5. Describe how to use the labor of a project team most efficiently.
6. Evaluate a lesson of your choice, using one of the critical thinking lessons as a model.

REFERENCES

Bloom, B. S.; Englehart, M. D.; Furst, E. J.; Hill, W. K.; & Krathwohl, R. R. *Taxonomy of Educational Objectives, Handbook I: Cognitive Domain.* New York: David McKay, 1956.

Cawelti, G. Address at the Sixth Annual Conference and Exhibition on Measurement and Evaluation; Pasadena, California (1979).

Lampert, S.; Wulf, K.; & Yanow, G. "A Solar Energy Curriculum for Elementary Schools," University of Southern California Progress Report, No. 1-EY-76-5-03-0113.

Los Angeles City Schools Instructional Planning Division, Programs for Gifted Section, *Critical Thinking Processes,* 1975.

McNeil, J. *Curriculum: A Comprehensive Introduction.* Boston: Little, Brown, 1981.

Oliva, P. *Developing the Curriculum*. Boston: Little, Brown, 1982.

Taba, H. *Curriculum Development: Theory and Practice*. New York: Harcourt, Brace, and World, 1962.

CHAPTER 8

ORGANIZING INSTRUCTIONAL MATERIALS

Don't reinvent the wheel.

Anonymous

Don't even reinvent any spokes if you can help it.

Kathleen M. Wulf

Once the lessons have been written, the project team members are entitled to feel a well-earned sense of accomplishment. They now have a group of lessons based on specific objectives based on clearly stated goals. Any teacher using one of the lessons can readily see by the coding letter and number the precise objective or objectives to be achieved by the learners. The purpose of this chapter is to provide the teacher with appropriate materials to help the student achieve the objectives in each lesson. The project team will take five major steps within this task:

1. Make a "shopping list" of materials needed.
2. Research materials already available.
3. Generate glossary, tests, worksheets, charts, workbooks, textbooks, filmstrips, films, behavioral checklists, and demonstration equipment.
4. Evaluate materials.
5. Make recommendations for a pilot test.

MAKING THE SHOPPING LIST

A common mistake in organizing instructional materials is choosing interesting material and then attempting to build an appropriate lesson around it. Since we see materials as a support for the achievement of objectives, not as ends in themselves, the choice of materials has been reserved for this phase of curriculum development.

In the first task of listing the materials needed, each lesson-writing group can prepare a statement of what is needed to make the lessons work. They can quickly survey: the *conditions* part of each objective they addressed or the *materials* part of each lesson plan. Using an example from the critical thinking curriculum (1975), the materials needed are: descriptive paragraph for motivational purpose, copies of advertisements, globe of the world, maps of North and South America, books from the bibliography, and charts as in attachments 4, 5, and 6. The group considers which of these are present in the typical class classroom and therefore eliminates the globe, the maps, and the books from the list (See Appendix C).

FINDING WHAT IS AVAILABLE

After all subgroups have listed desired materials, the team researches what is available. If, for example, a large poster advertising trips from New York to San Francisco round the horn exists in a book, then permission can be sought from the publishers to reproduce it. A primary rule is never to design a material if one already exists. Available sources from research are film catalogs, libraries, textbooks, old curricular materials, and picture and testing files. Again, this task is accomplished most expeditiously if each lesson design team seeks its own materials. Who knows better than they what they intended in the lesson?

GENERATING NEW MATERIALS

The third step is to generate the necessary materials still on the list after the research. Before anyone designs any material, however, agreement must occur regarding how much or how many resources can be allocated to the problem. Questions like these must be answered:

- Are we going to write a textbook?
- Did your group offer to make the demonstration devices?
- Is there anybody who can do the art work?
- How do you make a filmstrip?
- If we can't have all the materials we want, which ones will have to go?

These are critical reality questions. If there are economic constraints—for example, funds to make only *one* filmstrip—then plans need to be made to use that filmstrip to meet the objectives for as many lessons as possible. Similarly, if funds for consultants are limited, they must be used to hire talent not already present among the group members (e.g., artist, film maker, or equipment builder). If funds are limited, substitutions can be made in the materials list—for example, single lesson handout instead of workbook.

Despite such cuts, the group members keep one criterion before them: *teachers do not use lessons that are not complete.* Therefore, if cutting a particular learning material makes a lesson useless, it is important to change the conditions of the objectives and the activities to achieve the same end through less expensive means. The primary consideration is to select the best possible strategy and medium that will most effectively present the lesson.

After some healthy give-and-take, a final list of materials is agreed upon. Again, we recommend that each lesson-writing team prepare its own material. If there is expertise within the group, materials can be produced according to categories; one group writes all the test items, another group prepares the glossary, and a third group works with film media. All groups work from the lesson plans, reading the entire lesson to understand the intent or aim.

The first material to be developed, if not already uncovered in the research step, is a glossary of terms. As soon as this is prepared, it is shared immediately with the other project teams. Agreement upon terms in all phases of the curriculum is a fundamental need.

TEST CONSTRUCTION

Following the creation of a glossary, the test construction begins. With an instructional objectives method of curriculum design such as ours, each objective is itself a test item. Even though it is likely that not every lesson requires a written test, it is appropriate to prepare test items for each objective in each lesson, particularly for use as a pre-test. If more than one test item is written for each objective, these can become an "item bank" where the teacher can select randomly for pre-test and post-test items.

A pre-test is useful for each lesson, chiefly because it can identify those students who have acquired the behaviors necessary for completing the lesson. A post-test confirms that the learner has acquired the new behavior.

Test items can be produced as short fill-in answer style, or they can be created in other objective and essay formats.

Some valuable advice for test constructors is to consider decisions about what kinds of test items will most effectively measure the objectives. Different forms of test items may be used to cause students to demonstrate various kinds of behavior. Variations in design of the test items furnish opportunities for different levels of an examinee's response to emerge—for example, from Bloom's (1956) knowledge level through the hierarchy to the evaluation level.

Tests used in class are frequently of the paper-pencil format, either essay or objective. The essay examination requires a written response of a number of sentences in answer to a question or parts of a question. Each question can be developed from a parent behavioral objective. An "objective test," on the other hand, refers to an examination in which the marking process is the same for all student responses. This means that the appropriate responses have been agreed upon in advance and a scoring key prepared accordingly. Thus, regardless of who checks the answers, the method is "objective." Table 8.1 shows major differences between essay and objective tests.

There are four commonly used formats of objective tests: simple completion items, true-false items, multiple-choice questions, and matching exercises.

Simple Completion Tests

Simple completion items, often known as short answers and "fill-in-the-blanks," usually require students to respond in one- to ten-word answers. They often test recall at Bloom's knowledge level, but they can require more cognitively sophisticated answers at the application or synthesis levels.

Completion items are written as statements with a blank space where the student must insert a word or phrase. To avoid confusion, the blank should be at the end of the sentence rather than in the middle. Here is an example: "The author of *The Taxonomy of Educational Objectives: Cognitive Domain* is _____." Such completion items are useful in that they are not difficult to construct, they provide an efficient means of rapid coverage of content objectives, they allow for a divergent response, and they are more rapidly and reliably scored than essay examinations.

True-False Tests

True-false items are statements that students must judge to be more nearly true than false or more nearly false than true. They are used most frequently to test recognition at the knowledge level.

True-false items are used more often by classroom teachers than by developers of standardized tests. A typical true-false item is a statement or sentence which the student must judge to be correct or incorrect. Unlike a completion item, however, a true-false item requires some more complicated test construction skills. Wilson, Robeck, and Michael (1969) in their chapter on testing recommend these procedures:

1. Use definite and precise words so that the true-false item will be as simple and clear as possible.

TABLE 8.1
Summary of Major Differences Between Essay and Objective Tests

	Essay	Objective
Abilities measured	Requires the student to express himself in his own words, using information from his own background and knowledge.	Requires the student to select correct answers from given options or to supply an answer limited to one word or phrase.
	Can tap high levels of reasoning such as required in inference, organization of ideas, comparison and contrast.	Can also tap high levels of reasoning such as required in inference, organization of ideas, comparison and contrast.
	Does not measure purely factual information efficiently.	Measures knowledge of facts efficiently.
Scope	Covers only a limited field of knowledge in any one test. Essay questions take so long to answer that relatively few can be answered in a given period of time. Also, the student who is especially fluent can often avoid discussing points of which he is unsure.	Covers a broad field of knowledge in one test. Since objective questions may be answered quickly, one test may contain many questions. A broad coverage helps provide reliable measurement.
Incentive to pupils	Encourages pupils to learn how to organize their own ideas and express them effectively.	Encourages pupils to build up a broad background of knowledge and abilities.
Ease of preparation	Requires writing only a few questions for a test. Tasks must be clearly defined, general enough to offer some leeway, specific enough to set limits.	Requires writing many questions for a test. Wording must avoid ambiguities and "giveaways." Distractors should embody most likely misconceptions.
Scoring	Usually very time-consuming.	Can be scored quickly.
	Permits teachers to comment directly on the reasoning processes of individual pupils. However, an answer may be scored differently by different teachers or by the same teacher at different times.	Answer generally scored only right or wrong, but scoring is very accurate and consistent.

From *Making the Classroom Test: A Guide for Teachers,* Educational Testing Service Evaluation and Advisory Series, No. 4, © by Educational Testing Service, 1st ed. 1959, 2d ed. 1961.

2. Devise statements for true-false items that express one central thought or idea. In other words, "double-barreled" questions should be avoided.

3. Avoid the use of words known as specific determiners or cues, such as "always," "all," "never," "none," "impossible," or "without doubt," for such expressions are usually associated with items that are probably false. On the other hand, qualifying expressions such as "usually," "frequently," "sometimes," or "seldom" can create difficulties, as they are usually associated with items keyed as true.

4. Whenever possible, try to prepare items that are either completely true or completely false; that is, phrase the items so that there would be unanimous agreement among experts regarding whether the answer is true or false.

5. Prepare statements that are grammatically correct so that the conscientious student does not mark it false because of an inaccuracy in expression rather than because of an intentional inaccuracy of fact.

6. Write statements that stress main points or ideas rather than trivial details, "glittering generalities," or empty phrases.

7. Avoid, wherever possible, the use of negative expressions involving the insertion of the word "not," when otherwise the expression would have been precisely the opposite answer. In particular, avoid the use of double negatives, which are highly confusing and distracting.

8. Whenever an item deals with a controversial matter, the person, institution, or group that subscribes to that point of view should be named.

9. Endeavor to write statements that encourage students to apply whatever knowledge they have.

10. Include enough specific material so that the examinees do not have to depend upon their own opinions to determine what the intended meaning of the item might be.

11. Avoid taking material verbatim from the text and inserting it within an item; each item should be completely reworded to express the intended point or objective to be covered.

Just as in the completion format, there are advantages to true-false items. In the first place, the true-false test is a simple and direct means for assessing a student's knowledge of factual information. Secondly, it is efficient, capable of dealing with a great deal of material in a short testing time. Finally, many true-false items can be produced quickly. According to Wilson, Robeck, and Michael (1969), teachers can probably write at least 10 true-false items in the time it would take to write one multiple-choice question involving four or five alternatives.

Multiple-Choice Tests

Multiple-choice is the favored format of many testing experts. A multiple-choice item consists of a question or an introductory statement or stem, followed by two to five alternatives in parallel language, one alternative of which is the best or "truest" answer. The parallel language requires similar sequence and similar noun and verb structure, prepositional phrases, or complete sentences. This is a good example of alternatives parallel in structure:

> A UCS should do which of the following previous to conditioning?
> 1. Elicit the CS under investigation.
> 2. Elicit the UCR under investigation.
> 3. Elicit competing responses.
> 4. Elicit the CR.

It is important that each incorrect alternative, or distractor, be written so as to appear plausible or possibly true to the student. That is, if the multiple-choice format is to achieve its purpose, then all choices must be equally attractive to the student. Also, just as in the preparation of true-false items, one must keep in mind to avoid giving clues to the student through grammatical structure.

The primary advantage of the multiple-choice format is that the student can demonstrate behavior on high levels of thinking. Beyond that, another advantage is that students are required to make finer discriminations in their responses to the various alternatives than they would in the all-or-nothing task inherent in a true-false item. Similarly, the number of possible incorrect answers is vastly increased over a true-false test, where guessing might be expected to result in a score of 50 percent. In a multiple-choice test, with five alternatives for each item, an expected chance score is only 20 percent.

Matching Exercises

The last popular form of objective testing is that of matching items. Matching exercises include items of a given list to be placed in correspondence with one of several items of another list. The student is confronted with two sets of data, one as stimuli and one as responses. Items in each set, written as words, phrases, or sentences, are placed in correspondence with members from the second set, which may also be in words, phrases, or sentences. The student can be directed to use all answers when both sets are equal; or, when sets are not equal, to use some answers more than once or some not at all. For example:

Directions: *Write the letter corresponding to the country and insert in the space in front of the city named. A given country can be used more than once.*

_____	1.	Dusseldorf	A. United States
_____	2.	Buenos Aires	B. India
_____	3.	Casablanca	C. Germany
_____	4.	Bangkok	D. Brazil
_____	5.	Kathmandu	E. Morocco
_____	6.	Sarasota	F. Thailand
_____	7.	Rio de Janeiro	G. Nepal
_____	8.	Reno	H. Argentina
_____	9.	Calcutta	
_____	10.	Bonn	

Like multiple-choice items, matching can require students to employ higher thinking processes.

EVALUATION IN PRIMARY GRADES

Resultant tests can be evaluated by the project team using Tuckman's (1975) Checklist for Criterion-Referenced Tests (See Figure 8.1).

Worksheets and charts can be derived from objectives in each lesson using test items written in the preceding step. Any pertinent diagrams or pictorial work must be assigned for inclusion before the worksheet or chart is considered finished. In the case of the Model Lesson for Middle Grades found in Appendix C, two advertisements and three charts are required. The two advertisements, as suggested earlier, might be reproduced from books with permission of publishers, while the charts can be designed by the curriculum project team and attached directly to the lesson. Again, providing maximum use in the classroom is the goal. Therefore, it is desirable to provide as many camera-ready materials as possible, rather than concentrating on transparencies for overhead projectors.

Workbooks can be developed as a series of worksheets together; but textbooks, films, and demonstration or laboratory equipment might require the design help of an outside expert. To save on consultant time, it is appropriate to isolate specific lessons, complete with objectives, which need special materials. Then, combining their requirements contributes to the design of fewer and more universally applied learning aids. In the solar energy curriculum, for example, needs were combined so that only one filmstrip was required to facilitate learning of the Concept Area A goals: What is the sun? How does it work? What is solar energy?

FIGURE 8.I
Checklist for Criterion-Referenced Tests

I. IS MY TEST APPROPRIATE?
    1. Does it fit my objectives:
        a. Are there 2 items or more for each and every objective and 0 items that fit no objectives?
        b. Do the number of items per objective accurately reflect the relative importance of each objective?
    2. Does it reflect the action verbs:
        a. Does each item for a given objective measure the action called for by the verb in that objective?
        b. Have I used the item forms most appropriate for each action?
    3. Does it utilize the conditions:
        a. Does each item for a given objective employ the statement of givens or conditions set forth in that objective?
    4. Does it employ the criteria:
        a. Is the scoring of each item for a given objective based on the criteria stated in that objective?

II. IS MY TEST VALID?
    1. Does it discriminate between performance levels:
        a. Do students who are independently judged to perform better in the test area perform better on the test?
        b. Do different students with different degrees of experience perform differently on the various items?
    2. Does it fit any external criterion:
        a. Does success on the test predict subsequent success in areas for which the test topic is claimed to be a prerequisite?
        b. Do students who receive appropriate teaching perform better on the test than untaught students (or does a student perform better on the test after teaching than before)?
    3. How do my colleagues view the coverage:
        a. Do my colleagues in the topic area or at the grade level agree that all necessary objectives and no unnecessary ones have been included?
        b. Do they agree that the items are valid for measuring the objectives?
    4. Does it measure something other than reading level or lifestyles:
        a. Are the demands it makes on reading skill within students' capabilities?
        b. Is performance independent of group membership or any other socioeconomic variable?

III. IS MY TEST RELIABLE?
    1. Are there paired items that agree:
        a. Do students who get one item of a pair (per objective) right also get the other right and those who get one wrong get the other wrong?
        b. Have nonparallel items been rewritten?
    2. Is item performance consistent with test performance?
        a. Is each item consistently passed by students who do well on the total test?
        b. Have inconsistent items been removed?

3. Are all items clear and understandable:
   a. Have student responses been used as a basis for evaluating item clarity?
   b. Have ambiguous items been removed or rewritten?
4. Have scoring procedures proved to be systematic and unbiased:
   a. Have multiple scorings yielded consistent results?
   b. Are scoring criteria and procedures as detailed and as suitable as they can be?

IV. IS MY TEST INTERPRETABLE?
1. Do I know how the scores relate to relevant performance:
   a. Is my test referenced in terms of some criterion (e.g., my objectives)?
   b. Can I tell what a high score and a low score mean? Or can I report the specific objectives on which proficiency has been demonstrated?
   c. Can the results for an individual student be used as a specific indication of level or degree of proficiency?
2. Do I know what defines acceptable performance:
   a. Have I pre-established cutoff scores (e.g. passing grade), and if so, on what basis?
   b. Do I have some concrete and verifiable way to say whether a particular performance suffices in terms of objective specifications of acceptability?
3. Does the test provide diagnostic and evaluative information:
   a. Does it tell me the areas in which a student needs help?
   b. Does it tell me the areas in which the class needs help?
   c. Does it tell me the areas in which instruction needs improvement?
4. Does it provide useful relative information:
   a. Does it provide the kind of data I can compare meaningfully with results of past and future testings?
   b. Can the results be interpreted on a norm-referenced basis if that is desired?

V. IS MY TEST USABLE?
1. Is it short enough to avoid being tedious:
   a. Does it stop short of creating fatigue? stress? boredom?
   b. Have I tried to make it as short as possible within the limits of reliability?
2. Is it practical for classroom use:
   a. Can it be used conveniently in a classroom?
   b. Is it within the limit of available teacher time?
   c. Can it be used to test all students?
   d. Is it realistic about the kinds of equipment and physical setup it requires?
3. Are there standard procedures for administration:
   a. Are there clear, written instructions?
   b. Can it be administered by someone other than me?
   c. Can it be given in a nonthreatening, nondiscriminatory way?
4. Can students comprehend it and relate to it:
   a. Is it written at a level students can understand?
   b. Is it interesting, clever, or provocative?
   c. Is it written to engage students?

From B. W. Tuckman, *Measuring Educational Outcomes: Fundamentals of Testing* (New York: Harcourt Brace Jovanovich, 1975).

EVALUATING THE MATERIALS

When all of the materials are prepared and assembled for use, the project team again regroups for the analytical task of applying criteria and making judgments. In the case of materials, evaluation must be even more careful than in earlier steps in this design process, primarily because an attractive material may not be as good as it looks. More specifically, a material may be creative, intriguing, and fun, but if it does not help the student to achieve an objective, it must be replaced. Therefore, to aid in the appraisal of the instruction materials, the use of Eash's (1970) Instrument for the Assessment of Instructional Materials Form (IV) is recommended (See Appendix D).

MAKING RECOMMENDATIONS FOR PILOT TEST

Once the materials have been evaluated by the writing team, the final task is to make recommendations for the use of the whole learning package in its pilot test. The team members now have in hand a curriculum in its infancy. It possesses a whole body—all of the right parts—but it needs help as it emerges into the world. What should potential users know? What does the development team want from them? Can they be useful in helping to validate the lessons?

Each lesson in its final form with accompanying materials needs to be validated. Does the lesson actually teach what it is intended to teach? Methods of validation are varied: teacher evaluation, student achievement, student self evaluation. However, most frequently a post-test containing criterion test items is administered. Each learner demonstrates that he has attained the objectives by passing the criterion test. Standards for passing the test must be set by the teacher before the initial student tryout is conducted. Analysis of student performance data will enable the project team to assess how the lesson works.

If the project team wants such feedback from pilot test users, appropriate materials *must* accompany each lesson, and an overall statement enlisting the professional help of the teacher-users must precede the package. A concise one-page list of recommendations can explain as well as enlist support.

SUMMARY

The recommendations culminate the work done in this phase of organizing instructional materials. Earlier steps were: making a list of necessary materials, researching available materials, generating instructional aids, evaluating materials, and preparing recommendations for pilot tests.

FOLLOW-UP ACTIVITIES

1. Apply Tuckman's criteria to a teacher-written test for classroom use.
2. Research curriculum materials already existing in a subtopic of your area of interest. Make a bibliography of the various media and print resources available.
3. Apply Eash's criteria in evaluating one of the curricular pieces — for example, a text or workbook found in the course of your research (See No. 2 above).
4. Make a list of materials needed for all lessons.
5. Find material already available.
6. Prepare a plan for generating all necessary materials.
7. Use an evaluation instrument to appraise the quality of materials.
8. State recommendations for pilot testing.

REFERENCES

Bloom, B. S.; Engelhart, M. D.; Furst, E. J.; Hill, W. K.; & Krathwohl, D. R. *Taxonomy of Educational Objectives, Handbook I: Cognitive Domain*. New York: David McKay, 1956.

Eash, M. J. "Developing an Instrument for the Assessment of Instructional Materials (Form IV)." Paper read at Annual Convention of American Educational Research Association, 1970, Minneapolis.

Educational Testing Service Evaluation and Advisory Services, No. 4, *Making the Classroom Test: A Guide for Leaders*. Princeton, N.J.: Educational Testing Service, 1959, 1961, 1973.

Lampert, S.; Wulf, K.; & Yanow, G. "A Solar Energy Curriculum for Elementary Schools," University of Southern California Progress Report No. 1-EY-76-5-03-0113.

Los Angeles City Schools Instructional Planning Division, Programs for Gifted Section, *Critical Thinking Processes*, 1975.

Tuckman, B. W., A Checklist for Criterion-Referenced Tests. *Measuring Educational Outcomes: Fundamentals of Testing*. New York: Harcourt Brace Jovanovich, 1975.

Wilson, J. A. R., Robeck, M. C., & Michael, W. B. *Psychological Foundations of Learning and Teaching*. New York: McGraw-Hill, 1974.

CHAPTER 9

RECOMMENDING A LEARNING ENVIRONMENT

Left to themselves, things go from bad to worse.

Murphy's Law #5

At this point in our sequential model of curriculum development, the structure of the content, the goals, the instructional objectives, the lesson plans, and the appropriate materials have been carefully selected. The curriculum has been given a workable format. The curriculum designers must now be aware of the reality that the same curriculum can be presented in a variety of ways. In other words, curriculum that has been designed by the team will take on different characteristics depending on the learning environment that is chosen.

For the most successful use of the lessons and materials already developed, the team members need to recommend the optimal learning environment. An important consideration is not to take anything for granted. Often the first use of a new curriculum is by its developers, who intuitively know what type of learning environment was intended.

The crucial issue in this chapter is that provision must be made for the second generation of users. If recommendations about best environments do not accompany the lessons, accurate replication of the lessons is unlikely. A real-life example that characterizes this problem is found in the story of a famous French chef who prepared a recipe for a special cake but omitted information about what size cake pan to use and how to serve it. His assistants were confused when they had to make the cake on their own.

The purpose of this chapter is to help the team members implement in the most effective manner the materials chosen. Different facets of the learning environments will be described. Specifically, the physical, social, and psychological aspects of the learning environment will be delineated and implications for instruction considered.

THE PHYSICAL ENVIRONMENT:
THE HEIGHT AND WIDTH OF CURRICULUM

The actual physical environment—light, heat, spacing, seating arrangements, and learning centers—affects the quality of learning (Dunn & Dunn 1978). This fact is well accepted by teachers of early childhood education and elementary education. However, the concern for the physical environment seems to diminish as students get older. Nevertheless, the need for an appropriate physical environment does not diminish. Adolescents and adults learn better in environments that suit the needs of the learners.

It is the task of the team members to decide how the physical aspects of their learning environment will be structured. Questions about the amount of financial support necessary and the time required for construction or reconstruction in terms of work hours needed should be answered at this point.

If the new curriculum is designed for an existing school site, the following questions need to be addressed: Are we going to build a new school or a new classroom? Which room in our school is best suited for our purposes? What needs to be done to make the physical structure of the room more appropriate for our new curriculum? How much time will it take to make the changes? Who will be in charge? How will the work be divided up?

For example, in the solar energy curriculum (See Appendix A) it was decided that both indoor and outdoor environments would be required. Rooms with windows, preferably not basement classrooms, were necessary, as well as safe outdoor work spaces on the roof or on the playground for solar cooking and other sun experiments.

Another example of a design for a physical environment was the plan for the parent-infant-toddler program described earlier. Although the team members would have liked to have designed an indoor-outdoor environment specifically to meet the needs of infants and toddlers, the funds were not available. Team members were able to choose between two rooms in the school, a large upstairs adult classroom and a smaller downstairs preschool classroom. The preschool classroom was chosen because it had furniture, sinks, and bathrooms for children.

The room was designed to make the optimal use of the space available. The center of focus in the room was a carpeted area where parents and children could meet for discussions and play. Two child-size tables with chairs for cooking and art activities were set up. Empty walls were covered with blank paper for drawing. Shelves were used for the blocks, puzzles, puppets, and dolls used in the classroom.

Seating arrangements for the above-described programs were nontraditional. Seating in a traditional classroom is another variable in the physical environment. Often seating arrangements are the only aspects of the physical environment that can realistically be changed. Depending upon the task to be completed, choices of seating arrangements need to be explored. If, for example, the lesson requires an individual, introspective, written activity, the best organization would likely be straight rows or separate study spaces where interruption or distraction is minimal. However, if group discussion or problem solving is involved, then a horseshoe arrangement where all participants can see each other is necessary.

Other aspects of the physical environment from wall coverings to special equipment are left up to the imagination of the curriculum team. They must be attended to when recommending a learning environment.

THE SOCIAL ENVIRONMENT: THE INTERACTIVE CURRICULUM

Whether the teacher is modeling behaviors that are to be learned (i.e., physical movement, language, prosocial behavior, or nonaggressive behavior) or eliciting interactive responses, the social environment is a critical factor in learning.

Modeling

Bandura (1969) has written extensively on the role of modeling behaviors in the classroom. Modeling according to social learning theory is defined as imitative learning that occurs in a naturalistic social situation. Although the research on modeling is recent and application to the classroom situation is limited, this research strongly suggests that the teacher's behavior is modeled (imitated) for better or worse. In other words, actions speak louder than words. Research also indicates that nurturant or positive interaction between the student and the teacher increases the possibility of learning through modeling.

The team members need to decide to what extent modeling should be employed in their instructional design. For example, language courses, exercise and dance classes, and the behaviors of cooperation and nonviolence are taught primarily through modeling.

In the parent-infant-toddler program modeling played a critical role in two facets of the curriculum. Both language and nonabusive discipline were modeled by the teacher. In the solar energy curriculum modeling was used in lessons on the use of the scientific method. Teachers demonstrated how one predicts an outcome, forming hypotheses. Teachers showed how to construct equipment—for example, a solar hot dog cooker.

The choice as to the amount of modeling to be used in the classroom is up to the team members. However, curriculum designers should be aware that the teacher is always modeling personal attitudes toward the learning process to the students.

Group Interaction

The teacher decides how much group interaction to elicit from the students. Traditional views of education upheld the belief that student-teacher interactions were the most critical. However, recent research suggests student-student interactions contribute very significantly to the cognitive and social development of the child, the adolescent, the young adult, and the adult (Johnson 1980). Through peer interaction, psychological health is maintained, aggressive impulses are properly contained, social competence is learned, perspective taking is acquired, sex role identity is developed, and educational aspirations and achievement are influenced.

How much group interaction is possible within the structure of the content? This is the question curriculum planners must evaluate. Do goals of the curriculum allow for a great deal of peer interaction? How important is competition to the implementation of the curriculum? Is the curriculum so individualized that peer interaction is unnecessary? Consideration of the variable of peer interaction will affect the implementation of the curriculum that has been designed.

In the critical thinking curriculum, group interaction was an important part of the lessons' success. In the "Model Lesson for Primary Grades" (See Figure 7.4, in Chapter 7) the objective was: "Given a set of blocks of various shapes, sizes, and colors, the learner will discover . . . a 'given' premise. The premise is that only brown squares (any size, any thickness) may be buildings in 'My City.' " The children must be grouped so they all can see the "city" space—a circle made with six feet of string; as each child offers a block, the teacher emphasizes that only "buildings" of a certain size, shape, or color can be allowed in the city. Only through observing other children and the blocks accepted or rejected by the teacher can the individual learner achieve the objective of discovering the premise.

In the parent-infant-toddler program group interaction was a very necessary aspect of the curriculum design. Although the goal of group interaction did not have a specific purpose as in the critical thinking lesson, the feelings and thoughts of the group members served as the basis of the discussions about child development. The goals of the group discussion and the group interaction were to meet the needs of the learners, which is the possibility available when group interaction is an instructional technique.

THE PSYCHOLOGICAL ENVIRONMENT:
MATCHING THE LEARNING WITH THE LEARNER

The basic premise of our approach is that curriculum to be effective should be designed for a specific group of learners. Now the curriculum team must take this maxim one step further and consider the psychological components of learning. The behavioral and cognitive theories of learning presented here suggest how people acquire new information and new skills. The theorists see learning from different perspectives, which imply different appropriate methodologies. For example, a cognitive theorist would differ from a behaviorist not only on the nature of learning but also on the process and products of learning. It is up to the team members to agree as to which learning theory and strategies is most valuable to the implementation of their curriculum.

Behavioral Theory:
"The Objective Aspect of Learning"

Behavioral theorists such as Skinner, Watson, Thorndike, and Guthrie have formalized and made operational principles of learning. These principles are based upon experimental research in laboratory settings with both animals and humans. Behaviorists describe how behavior is learned in terms of primary and secondary drives.

Primary drives are defined as principles of association which state that learning occurs when a stimulus is presented and a response is elicited. Pavlov's classic example of the dog hearing the bell, being given the meat, and then salivating is representative of this principle. Secondary-drive principles of reinforcement state that learning occurs after a response that makes it more likely to occur. This principle of reinforcement is a broader way of describing learning by means of an established reward system, which may be material, psychological, or physical.

According to the behavioral theorists, learning is a stimulus-response activity. The learner is exposed to a designated stimulus that elicits a specific response or a specific reinforcer. The behaviorists postulate that the learner should be reinforced appropriately and systematically for desirable responses. Repetition of stimulus responses (s-r bonds), often labelled overlearning, actively assures retention of new materials. Trial and error is a part of the learning process which assumes that "habits of acquisition" are acquired in this way. One situation where stimulus-response learning might be desirable is in the case of drills for basic math facts (e.g., times tables).

Transfer of knowledge, labeled generalization and discrimination, involves practice in other contexts. Modeling is a tool used by behaviorists to teach behavior that cannot be learned by trial and error. Motivation for the behavioral theorists is external to the learner and thus extrinsic. The product of learning is observable and measurable (Bower & Hilgard 1975).

Behavioral theory has been criticized for being overly simplistic and incomplete. However, the behaviorist movement has helped educators identify the desired outcomes in clear and concise terms. It provides a technological structure of learning that assists in defining the goals, the objectives, and the evaluation of curriculum. Curriculum planners need to decide to what extent behaviorism is important to their goals. Technologically designed curriculum relies heavily on these strategies. In other words, if the outcomes of learning are measurable, then the principles of behaviorism may be applied to the classroom.

Cognitive Theory: "The Subjective Dimension"

Cognitive field psychology emphasizes the perceptual field of the learner in the learning process in direct opposition to the behaviorists' incremental theory of stimulus response. Cognitive psychologists view the whole learning process as being greater than the sum of its parts. For the purposes of curriculum designers using our text, the cognitive field theories of Piaget, Bruner, and Ausubel will be reviewed.

Piaget (1958), a cognitive developmental theorist with Inhelder, points out that for learning to be assimilated it should be aimed at the child's level of cognitive development. Piaget describes four stages of cognitive development that are contingent upon the child's maturation. These stages evolve from a sensory motor mode of learning of the infant, to the egocentric thought of the young child, to the concrete thinking of the school-age child, to the abstract thinking of the adolescent. Through the balancing (equilibration) of imitation (accommodation) and fantasy (assimilation), learners engage in activities that help them understand their own worlds (Piaget & Inhelder 1969).

Bruner (1960) extended the work of Piaget, who never actually worked on applying his theory of stages to learning. Bruner proposed a "spiral curriculum"—a curriculum that can present concepts in ways that are matched with the learner's cognition stage and thus maintains the interest of the learner. Bruner also suggested that readiness can be taught through working within the cognitive structure and extending it.

Piaget and Bruner advocate discovery learning. The learner is perceived as an active processor of information. The learner should be allowed to formulate problems or goals and search for alternative solutions rather than look for externally designated answers, as recommended by the behaviorists. The role of the teacher is to guide meaningful inquiry and to present material in an understandable manner, allowing the child to learn from personal experiences.

Ausubel (1965), like the other cognitive theorists, believes that all knowledge should be made meaningful to the learner. However, Ausubel is not concerned with discovery learning or learning as a process activity; rather, he addresses meaningful receptive learning, which should be used for practical instruction and lecturing.

In order for new material to be meaningful to the learner it must be attached to previous knowledge which will "anchor" the new knowledge in the mind of the learner. New material coming into cognitive structures is subsumed by existing ideas. Subject matter is the focus of this learning theory, which stresses organizational principles to insure meaningful learning.

According to Ausubel, introductory "advance organizers" are presented in advance of the actual learning to provide subconcepts that are anchors or reference points to aid the learner in subsuming new material. The most general and inclusive concepts should be taught first. Next, the less inclusive concepts are taught. Finally, specific details are presented.

The key to understanding this theory is to recognize that learning should be intrinsic, meaningful, and organized in such a way that the ideas presented will be related to the learner's experiences. In a lecture format, for example, Ausubel would recommend preparing the content flow so that new ideas could be "anchored" to existing concepts.

In summary, the cognitive theorists emphasize a learner's perceptual field or developmental stage or life space as an important variable in the learning environment. They are concerned with meaningful learning, intrinsic motivation, and the subjective aspects of learning. Inquiry, discovery, and problem-solving approaches are encouraged by these theorists. Curriculum planners must decide how the strategies of the cognitive theorists fit into their structure of the content. If subjective and process-orientated goals have been agreed upon, then the strategies of the cognitive theorists need to be carefully considered.

SUMMARY

This chapter addressed aspects of the learning environment, specifically the physical, social, and psychological. The team members must make definite recommendations to the curriculum users in order that the lessons and materials will be used most appropriately and effectively.

FOLLOW-UP ACTIVITIES

1. Describe three aspects of the physical learning environment.
2. Describe two aspects of the social learning environment.
3. Briefly compare and contrast behaviorist and cognitive theories of learning.

4. Using the lesson in Appendix C, prepare a short paragraph recommending a learning environment.
5. Explain how matching the learning environment with the learner is an important part of this process of curriculum design.
6. Explain how this chapter's tasks, recommending learning environments, contribute to the success of the finished curriculum.

REFERENCES

Ausubel, D. *Educational Psychology: A Cognitive View.* New York: Holt, Rhinehart & Winston, 1965.

Bandura, A. *Principles of Behavior Modification.* New York: Holt, Rhinehart & Winston, 1969.

Bower, G., & Hilgard, E. *Theories of Learning.* Englewood Cliffs, N.J.: Prentice-Hall, 1975.

Bruner, J. *The Process of Education.* Cambridge, Mass.: Harvard University Press, 1960.

Dunn, G., & Dunn, R. *Teaching Students Through Individual Learning Styles: A Practical Approach.* Reston, Va.: Reston Publishing, 1978.

Johnson, J. "Group Processes: Influences of Student-Student Interaction on School Outcomes." In *School Psychology of School Learning.* New York: Academic Press, 1980.

Piaget, J., & Inhelder, B. *The Growth of Logical Thinking from Childhood to Adolescence.* New York: Basic Books, 1958.

Piaget, J., & Inhelder, B. *The Psychology of the Child.* New York: Basic Books, 1969.

Smith, M. *Educational Psychology and Its Classroom Application.* Boston: Allyn & Bacon, 1975.

CHAPTER 10

DECIDING UPON EVALUATION

The first 90 percent of the task takes 90 percent of the time, and the last 10 percent takes the other 90 percent.

Ninety-ninety Rule of Project Schedules

Sadly, the "ninety-ninety rule" is often true. A good project team develops a curriculum to the point of testing the lesson material and recommending a learning environment, and then the program dies. Time is used up. The funding runs out. Innovative lessons are not disseminated for wider use, and the whole package is locked up in somebody's files. Without planned evaluation and feedback regarding a curriculum's effectiveness, its use beyond the developmental team members is severely limited.

Evaluation is essential for one fundamental reason: the project team needs to know if the curriculum works. If it doesn't, they can take the appropriate feedback to whatever step is appropriate — goals, objectives, materials, or learning environment — and improve the project for the next iteration. In our model, provision for change and modification is built in from the beginning. Relevant feedback, both positive and critical, is expected, not feared.

DESIGNING AN EVALUATION PLAN

By far the most difficult part of evaluation is deciding what questions to ask. Selecting evaluation instruments, collecting data, and analyzing the data are much less time-consuming than this preliminary stage of writing questions. What do we want to know about our lessons? Whose opinions do we want to look at — parents'? teachers'?

school administrators'? Are we interested in student achievement in the new concept areas, or are we more concerned about attitude change? Do we wish to compare our curriculum with a similar one? What did our goals say we were trying to achieve?

Discussion among the entire project team will result in identification of several questions which need to be answered in a pilot test before the curriculum can be shared on a wider scale. The team members will select appropriate strategies for answering those questions. Such forms of evaluation might include student achievement tests (already prepared within the materials package), student attitude surveys, student self-appraisal surveys, parent opinion devices, teacher comments, teacher anecdotal records, teacher checklists, and norm-referenced tests. Table 10.1, from Issac and Michael (1977), lists types of behaviors or learning outcomes with possible methods of evaluation.

FORMATIVE AND SUMMATIVE EVALUATION

Regardless of one's philosophic orientation toward schools and learning, curriculum evaluation always must investigate two major questions: Do planned learning opportunities as developed and organized actually produce desired results? How can the curriculum offerings best be improved?

Since the answers to these questions require a process of decision making, it is necessary that the evaluation provide enough of the appropriate information. It might require two kinds of evaluation. Whereas *formative evaluation* is intended to improve an existing program, *summative evaluation* is done to assess the effect of a completed program.

Formative Evaluation

Cronbach (1963) offered these suggestions for conducting formative evaluation:

1. Seek data regarding changes produced in pupils by the course.
2. Look for multidimensional outcomes and separately map out the effects of the course along these dimensions.
3. Identify aspects of the course in which revisions are desirable.
4. Collect evidence midway in curriculum development while the course is still fluid.
5. Try to find out how the course produces its effect and what influences its effectiveness. You may find that the teacher's attitude toward the learning opportunity is more important than the opportunity itself.

TABLE 10.1
Table of Representative Learning Outcomes
and Possible Methods of Evaluation

(Numbers in parentheses refer to code designation taken from *Instructions for Title 1 1967 Application Forms OE-37003*, page 13.)

A Application (11–14) Concept Acquisition (11–14) Memorization of Facts (11–14) Problem Solving (11–14) Reading Comprehension (11–14) Skills (number, etc.) (11–14)	**A** Objective Test, Product Evaluation, Rating Scale, Checklist
B Performance (11)	**B** Rating Scale, Checklist, Product Evaluation
C Classroom Behavior (41–45)	**C** Rating Scale, Checklist, Attendance Record, etc.
D Interest (14)	**D** Questionnaire, Checklist, Interest Inventory, Factual Vocabulary Test (with words from various interest fields)
E Attitude (31, 32)	**E** Rating Scale, Questionnaire, Checklist, or Objective Test (with factual material that has attitude-loaded responses)
F Aspiration Level (33, 34)	**F** Rating Scale, Interview, Simple Objective Test, Word Association Test, Open-ended Sentences (psychologist needed)
G Adjustment (53)	**G** Rating Scale, Anecdotal Report, Interview, Sociogram

From *Handbook in Research and Evaluation* by Stephen Isaac in collaboration with William B. Michael. © 1977 by EdITS Publishers, San Diego.

6. During trial stages, use the teacher's informal reports of observed pupil behavior in aspects of the course.
7. Make more systematic observations only after the more obvious bugs in the early stages have been dealt with.
8. Make a process study of events taking place in the classroom and use proficiency and attitude measures to reveal changes in pupils.
9. Observe several outcomes ranging far beyond the content of the curriculum itself—attitudes, general understanding, aptitude for further learning.

Summative Evaluation

Summative evaluation, on the other hand, frequently requires comparative research designs. For example, while formative evaluation seeks to find out how a given set of lessons affects learners, summative evaluation often seeks to compare one program with another. In such evaluation studies, one curriculum is regarded as Treatment A and another as Treatment B (Campbell & Stanley 1963).

In comparing group performances, as is frequently necessary in summative evaluation, there are pitfalls. Horst and others of the RMC Research Corporation (1975) identified twelve hazards to conducting summative evaluations:

The use of grade-equivalent scores.   One should not use grade-equivalent scores in evaluating programs. The concept is misleading; a grade-equivalent score of seven by fifth graders on a math test does not mean that they know sixth- and seventh-grade math. Such scores do not comprise an equal interval scale; therefore, "average" scores make them too low in the fall and too high in the spring.

The use of gain scores.   Gain scores have been used to adjust for differences found in the pre-test scores of treatment and comparison groups. Using them in this way is a mistake because raw gain scores (post-test scores minus pre-test scores) excessively inflate the post-test performance measure of an initially inferior group. Students who initially have the lowest scores will have the greatest opportunity to show gain.

The use of norm-group comparisons with inappropriate test dates. A distorted picture of a program's effect occurs when pupils in the new program are not tested within a few weeks of the norm group's tests. Standardized test developers might collect performance scores in May for the purpose of norming the test. If the school's staff, however, administers the test during a different month, the discrepancy might be due to the date of testing rather than to the program.

The use of inappropriate test levels. Standardized norm-referenced tests are divided into levels that cover different grades. The test level may be too easy or too difficult and thereby fail to provide a valid measure of achievement. Ceiling and floor effects may also occur with the use of criterion-referenced tests. Hence, one should choose tests on the basis of the pupils' achievement level, not their grade in school.

The lack of pre- and post-test scores for each treatment participant. The group of students ultimately post-tested is not usually composed of exactly the same students as the pre-test group. Eliminating from the post-test the scores of dropouts may raise the post-test scores considerably. Conclusion of a program's report should be used on the performance of students who have both pre-test and post-test scores. The reason for student drop out should also be reported.

The use of noncomparable treatment and comparison groups. Students should be randomly assigned to groups. If they are not, students in a special program may do better or worse than those in other programs because they were different to start with.

Using pre-test scores to select program participants. Groups with low pre-test scores appear to learn more from a special program than they actually do because of a phenomenon called regression toward the mean. Gains of high-scoring students may be obscured.

Assembling a matched comparison group. The correct procedure for matching groups is to match pairs of pupils and then randomly assign one member of each pair to a treatment or comparison group. If, for example, one wants to control for age, one should choose pairs of pupils of the same age. Each member of the pair must have an equal opportunity to be assigned to a given treatment. Do not consciously try to place one member in a certain group.

Careless administration of tests. Pupils from both treatment and comparison groups should complete pre- and post-tests together. Problems arise when there is inconsistent administration of tests to the two groups. For example, if there is a disorderly teaching situation in one setting and an orderly teaching situation in the other, the results may differ because of the environments, not the students.

The assumption that an achievement gain is due to the treatment alone. The Hawthorne effect—unrecognized "treatments"—may be responsible for gain. Plausible rival hypotheses should be examined as a likely explanation for the results.

The use of noncomparable pre-test and post-test. Although there are conversion tables that allow one to correct scores on one test to their equivalent on other tests, it is best to use the same level of the same test for both pre- and post-test. Obviously, this will not suffice if teachers teach to the test and if there are practice effects from taking the test.

The use of inappropriate formulas to estimate post-test scores. Formulas that calculate "expected" post-test scores from I.Q. or on average grade-equivalent scores are inaccurate. The actual post-test scores of treatment and comparison groups provide a better basis for evaluating treatment effects.

MODELS OF EVALUATION

A number of theoreticians in curriculum development have established their own models of evaluation. A good textbook in curriculum philosophy and evaluation will compare and contrast their various advantages better than is possible here in one brief chapter. Most of these schemes do have in common two factors. First, they seek to determine how well a curriculum achieved its goals, and second, they seek to manage decision making within the process. A summary of prototypes of curriculum evaluation is presented in Table 10.2.

The model of evaluation advocated in our book is whatever one best fits the needs of the project team. The approach in the preceding chapters has already laid the groundwork for decision making by the development team. The feedback loops from each step back to earlier stages have facilitated the orderly systematic building of curriculum. Each step had its own evaluation component. Evaluation here is simply the last logical step to affirm the products of each stage.

Using the questions derived by the project team, suitable instruments must be chosen or developed. Like the issue of the instructional materials, the development of evaluation instruments is easier if the team begins with testing or appraisal scales already existing. In formative evaluation, in particular, instruments can be modified for another purpose. Following are some examples of evaluation instruments designed by project teams employing our approach or a similar approach.

First are three evaluation forms from the solar energy project. On the teacher evaluation (See Figure 10.1) the teacher had the opportunity to cite brief information plus a comment on how, in the teacher's professional opinion, the lesson might be improved.

Figure 10.2 shows a second evaluation instrument for the same program, to be used immediately after the solar energy lessons had been presented to the learners. Deliberately prepared for young learners, the response choices of "not much," "OK," and "a lot" were accompanied by "sad" and "happy" faces to facilitate students' understanding.

TABLE 10.2
Prototypes of Curriculum Evaluation*

Prototype Evaluation Procedure	Key Emphasis	Purpose	Key Activities	Key Viewpoint Used To Delimit Study
Ralph Tyler's Evaluation Model[1]	Instructional Objectives	To measure student progress toward objectives	Specify objectives; measure student competence	Curriculum Supervisor; Teacher
School Accreditation Model[2]	Staff Self Study	To review content and procedures of instruction	Discuss program; make professional judgments	Classroom Teacher; Administrator
Bob Stake's Countenance Model[3]	Description and Judgment Data	To report the ways different people see the curriculum	Discover what audience wants to know about; observe; gather opinions	Audience of final report
Dan Stufflebeam's CIPP Model[4]	Decision Making	To facilitate rational and continuing decision making	Identify upcoming alternatives; study implications; set up quality control	Administrator Director
Hilda Taba's Social Studies Evaluation Model[5]	Cause-and-Effect Relationships what works	To seek simple but enduring explanation of variation	Exercise experimental control and systematic	Theorist; Researcher

*Prepared by Robert E. Stake, CIRCE, University of Illinois, October, 1969 (mimeo).
References:
[1]Tyler, Ralph W. "General Statement on Evaluation." *Journal of Educational Research,* 35, (March 1942): 492–501.
[2]National Study of Secondary School Evaluation. *Evaluative Criteria.* 1980 Ed., Washington, D.C.: National Study of Secondary School Evaluation.
[3]Stake, Robert E. "The Countenance of Educational Evaluation." *Teachers College Record* 68, (April 1967): 523–40.
[4]Stufflebeam, Daniel L. "Evaluation As Enlightenment for Decision-making." The Evaluation Center (College of Education), Ohio State University, Columbus, Ohio 1967 (mimeo). To be published by Association for Supervision & Curriculum Development.
[5]Taba, Hilda. "Teaching Strategies and Cognitive Functioning in Elementary School Children." Cooperative Research Project No. 2404. San Francisco State College, San Francisco.

Outside Experts Needed	Expected Teaching Staff Involvement	Risks	Payoff
Objectives Specifiors; Measurement Specialists	Conceptualize objectives; give tests	Oversimplify school aims; ignore processes	Ascertain student progress
None; unless authentication by outside peers needed	Committee discussions	Exhaust staff; ignore values of outsiders	Increase staff leadership responsibility
Journalists; Social Psychologists	Keep logs; give opinions	Stir up value conflicts; ignore causes	Broad picture of curriculum and conflicting expectations
Operations Analysts	Anticipate decisions, contingencies	Overvalue efficiency, undervalue student aims	Curriculum sensitive to feedback
Research Designer; Statistical Analysts	Tolerate experimental constraints	Artificiality; ignore personal values	Gets rules for developing new programs

FIGURE 10.1
Teacher Evaluation of Solar Energy Lessons

TEACHER'S NAME _____ SCHOOL _____

GRADE OF LEARNERS _____

LESSON TAUGHT _____

TIME REQUIRED (i.e., hours or minutes) _____

LEARNER'S REACTION: Good _____ Fair _____ Poor _____

COMMENT: In my professional opinion, I feel that this lesson could be improved by

_____

_____

_____

_____

_____

The third form (See Figure 10.3) reflected an appraisal of one of the goals of the project: "the students understand energy conservation." To assess learning in the classroom, parents were asked to respond to two questions.

Another example of a student evaluation is that of Krop (1973) for use with graduate students in sociology (See Figure 10.4). Rather than testing knowledge of content, this instrument taps students' attitudes regarding the format of the lesson.

With mature respondents it is possible to ask many of the questions all at once. As part of a summative evaluation of one elementary school's program, this long parent questionnaire was designed (See Figure 10.5).

Frequently a quick evaluation format is the teacher or observer checklist (See Figure 10.6). This lists behaviors which the teacher or helper can quickly observe; for example, a check in column 2 indicates that the child responded verbally when asked questions about the lesson.

These half dozen examples were all designed by curriculum teams who began with the questions they needed to have answered. Attempts were made to keep the instruments as brief as possible and to provide opportunities for responses to be brief but meaningful. As a general rule in any questionnaire or survey technique, *keep the instrument as simple and short as possible.*

Four useful guidelines for preparing self-report and attitudinal devices have been given succinctly by Gottman and Clasen (1972):

• Be direct. Most tests can be "psyched-out."
• Be brief. If you ask one question, why use two?

FIGURE 10.2
Student Evaluation of Solar Energy Lessons

	Not Much	OK	A Lot
1. I thought the lessons were interesting.	_____	_____	_____
2. I understood the lessons on solar energy.	_____	_____	_____
3. I want to learn more about solar energy.	_____	_____	_____
4. I have already told my family about solar lessons we did in class.	_____	_____	_____

Teacher's Name_____

Grade Level_____

- Be simple. Complex questions result in complex answers.
- Be creative. Multiple choice is not the only possible way.

One form of evaluation that may be an exception to the above rules is the anecdotal record. Asking teachers or observers to comment in writing on a learner's behavior is a gruesome prospect *unless* there is structure to the evaluation. What behavior deserves comment? What changes are we looking for? What specifically are the objectives we're trying to achieve? If there are a number of behaviors that demonstrate the new learning, then the evaluation on task is to keep track of them in some orderly way.

If, for instance, the curriculum under evaluation includes multicultural experiences toward the goal of achieving greater acceptance of different ethnic groups, the use of anecdotal records of playmates chosen might be an outstanding choice of evaluation methodology. In using this format, however, it is imperative to set the structure for respondents carefully, explaining the kinds of behavior sought and providing a sample anecdotal record to use as a model. Then this type of evaluation can also conform to rules of directness, brevity, simplicity, and creativity.

Before the evaluation phase of the design process can be executed, the project team will determine if it has collected and prepared sufficient and appropriate instruments to answer the questions about the new curriculum. Are there ample tests of student

FIGURE 10.3
Parent Evaluation of Solar Energy Lessons

Teacher's Name _____

Grade Level_____

Dear Parent,

Would you be kind enough to help us evaluate our lessons in solar energy? We taught some new material to your youngster's class, and we want to see if the new knowledge was shared with you at home.

1. Did your son/daughter tell you that the class was
   studying solar energy?   Yes _____   No _____

2. Did your youngster talk about conserving energy in
   your home?   Yes _____   No _____

Thank you for your cooperation. Please return this form to the teacher.

---

achievement; teacher, administrator, 'parent, community opinion; student attitude—plus other evaluation devices? Are these materials in a format that the project team, as professionals, would be willing to use? Are there any ways that the instruments could be more finely tuned? Gronlund (1978) has prepared a checklist to help evaluate evaluation instruments (See Figure 10.7).

EVALUATION OF WHOM?

With evaluation materials ready to investigate responses to the questions which need to be answered, the project team decides upon the population it wishes to evaluate. Obviously, we cannot administer the new learning experiences and new evaluation instruments to all learners. Therefore, it is appropriate to select a sample of learners who represent the target population. Research design theory insists that a sample selected *randomly* has the advantages of greater generalizability of results and fewer threats to validity than a sample "rounded up" from friends and assorted volunteers. (A caution: Project team members themselves are in one sense a fine group of teachers to administer the pilot curriculum to their own students, because these teachers are experts in the materials; but precisely for this reason they are atypical, and their data should not be combined with that of classes whose teachers are new to the materials. Therefore, project team members should not be used in the pilot test.)

When selecting a sample for an evaluation of a new curriculum, it is important to identify the group for whom it is intended. Our examples of new curriculum in previous chapters showed a wide range of content and audience: educational training for Peace Corps teachers, critical thinking for the gifted, solar energy for elementary school children. Every curriculum has an expected audience, with some even more specifically defined (e.g., slow learning children in bilingual classrooms). Whatever the learners' category or label, a pilot test must, by design, address a sample of that population.

Before a sample can be selected, it is necessary to look at an important variable: availability. Will all the teachers we select be willing to try the new curriculum and share the results with us? Do we have the training program for vast numbers of participants? Are we able to deal with a wide geographic area? Sometimes the answers to these questions necessitate a narrowing of scope for pilot evaluation. Sometimes it means asking for volunteers to use the new curriculum in target areas, and then selecting randomly from those who are willing. In any case, the goal for the project team is to identify a sample from which generalizations can be made to the wider audience.

PREPARING FOR EVALUATION

Once the pilot test sample has been identified and the evaluation instruments are ready, the project team can prepare a time line which outlines the strategy for collecting these data. Often such a time line can be written "backwards"—that is, enter the final reporting date at the bottom of the page and space appropriate tasks in earlier time frames. This process is simply another sequencing of tasks.

As soon as the general time line is ready, letters can be drafted to the leaders of schools or groups that the team wishes to use in the sample. Such a letter explains the purpose of the pilot test and, equally important, asks for participation. (See Figure 10.8 for sample letter—the letter used in connection with the solar energy curriculum.)

Besides the agreement of local school administrators, however, it is often necessary to secure permission from district-level personnel. A brief letter describing the new materials, with copies of the proposed evaluation instruments, is appropriate. Large school districts frequently require any proposed testing of students, particularly in attitudinal areas, to pass a standing committee whose function is to protect students from being misused as human subjects. When consents are received, the evaluation plan can proceed to the inservice training of willing participants.

TRAINING FOR PILOT TEST

The purpose of inservice training is to acquaint the users with the curriculum. In planning to meet the sample participants for the first time, the project team can regard them as learners new to the materials. Goals and objectives for the inservice are set in advance, and ap-

FIGURE 10.4
Module Evaluation for Graduate Course in Sociology

Name:_____

If student, first year of graduate program   If you are a peer, are you:

_____   1. Classroom Instructor   _____
                                                 2. Student Supervisor   _____
Are you in second year of graduate   3. Practitioner   _____

program_____   What is your educational degree _____

This self-instructional unit utilizes the modern systems approach to education and applies it to social work field instruction. It is an approach to social work field teaching in which field work is conceptualized as a course for which behavioral objectives can be identified, content selected, learning opportunities planned, and student learning assessed.

Biestek's principles of relationship were chosen for this learning module because of their clarity and applicability. If it is determined that the modern systems approach to education enhances field work teaching, similar units will be constructed covering essential theories, principles, concepts, and techniques basic to social work practice.

The instructor wishes to determine whether a modern systems approach can be used as a rational framework to increase the effectiveness of teaching in social work field training. Some of the problems which have been identified are integrating classroom and field work instruction, providing an equal opportunity for basic field learning for students in diverse field placements, and promoting independence for the student in professional learning in the field.

After working through the unit, please give your responses to the following questions:

1. Do you feel that self-contained units of instruction such as the one you just completed:
   a. are useful in integrating class and field instruction by selecting and ordering learning content and experiences?
      Yes _____ No _____
      Please explain your answer.

   b. offer an approach by which an equal opportunity for basic field learning is provided for all students?
      Yes _____ No _____
      Comments:

   c. are useful in promoting greater independence for students in their own professional learning in the field?
      Yes _____ No _____
      Comments:

   d. would help alleviate field work instructor's anxiety about what and how to teach
      by establishing a structured pattern and plan for field learning?
      Yes _____ No _____
      Comments:

2. Can you suggest other ways that individualized instructional packages can enhance
   the effectiveness of social work field training?

REVISION

The instructor would like to improve this self-contained unit of instruction based on
your reactions to these questions:

1. Do you feel the material dealt with in this unit is relevant to your present or future
   needs? Yes _____ No _____

2. This self-instructional unit was purposely designed as a paper-and-pencil package.
   Would it have been more helpful to you to have a film tape of casework interviews
   as a learning activity instead of written interviews? Yes _____ No _____ Plus
   the written interviews? Yes _____ No _____

3. How much did you enjoy working through this unit?
   A lot _____ Some _____ Little _____ None _____

4. Do you feel the material presented in this unit was presented clearly and concisely?
   Yes _____ No _____
   If not, please go back and identify the sources of your confusion and explain them.

5. Did this unit help you to become more aware of your own behavior in professional
   and personal relationships? Yes _____ No _____

6. Which statements best describe your feelings about your involvement with this
   learning unit?

Too easy	_____	Boring	_____	Just another requirement	_____
Inspiring	_____	Helpful	_____		
A waste of time	_____	OK	_____	Others	_____
Interesting	_____	Too time consuming	_____		_____

FIGURE 10.5
Parent Questionnaire

We have a good educational program at _____ School; each year brings
new programs and personnel to make our school even better. We ask *your* help to further this improvement by taking the time to share with us your thinking about the
school. This is your opportunity to indicate areas of satisfaction and areas in which you
desire improvement. Thank you.

I. ACADEMICS

1. As a parent, do you feel you have been made aware of your child's academic
   strengths and weaknesses?
   Yes _____   No _____

2. The following are methods which may be used to inform you of your child's
   academic strengths and weaknesses. Please indicate their effectiveness this past
   semester.

	Very Effective	Moderately Effective	Ineffective
Parent-teacher conferences	_____	_____	_____
Informal discussions w/teachers	_____	_____	_____
Letters and phone calls	_____	_____	_____
Teacher comments on assigned work	_____	_____	_____

3. Do you feel your child's individual learning needs have been generally recognized?
   Yes _____   No _____   Sometimes _____

4. The following academic areas are found in all elementary school programs.
   Please indicate your evaluation of the emphasis in the following areas by checking the appropriate column.

This area was emphasized:

ACADEMIC AREA	TOO MUCH	ABOUT RIGHT	TOO LITTLE	NOT SURE
Language Arts: oral				
Language Arts: written				
Mathematics				
Music				
Art				
Physical Education				
Reading				
Science				
Social Studies (History, Geography, Current Events)				

5. Please evaluate your child's progress in the following academic areas:

This area was emphasized:

ACADEMIC AREA	TOO MUCH	ABOUT RIGHT	TOO LITTLE	NOT SURE
Language Arts: oral				
Language Arts: written				
Mathematics				
Music				
Art				
Physical Education				
Reading				
Science				
Social Studies (History, Geography, Current Events)				

6. Do you feel your child's work efforts have been evaluated adequately?
   Yes _____   No _____   Sometimes _____   Not Sure _____

7. Do you feel your child has been made aware of his or her academic strengths and weaknesses?
   Yes _____   No _____   Sometimes _____   Not Sure _____

8. Do you feel the school is helping your child develop independence and self-direction?
   Yes _____   No _____   Sometimes _____   Not Sure _____

9. Please rate your child's progress in independent learning and problem solving.
   Excellent _____   Fair/Good _____   Little or No Progress _____

10. Overall, are you satisfied with the academic program your child takes part in at school?
    Yes _____   No _____   Not Sure _____
    Please give your comments or recommendations regarding the academic aspects of the school program.

    _____

    _____

    _____

    _____

II. ATTITUDES
   1. Please rate your child's attitude toward school.
      Positive attitude _____   So-so attitude _____   Negative attitude _____

   2. Last year my child attended: This school _____   Another school _____
      My child's attitude toward school this year as compared to last year is:
      More positive _____   The same as last year _____   Less positive _____

   3. Do you feel your child knows what is expected of him or her in the following areas:
      Classroom standards of behavior?   Yes _____   No _____
      Academics?   Yes _____   No _____

   4. Do you feel classroom standards of behavior are:
      too free _____   about right _____   too rigid _____   not sure _____

5. Do you think your child feels comfortable in asking for help at school?
Yes _____ No _____ Not sure _____
When your child does ask for help, do you think it is usually provided?
Yes _____ No _____ Not sure _____ Sometimes _____

6. Do you feel that positive attitudes are being fostered in the following areas?

Self-respect	Yes _____	No _____	Not sure _____
Respect for peers	Yes _____	No _____	Not sure _____
Respect for adults	Yes _____	No _____	Not sure _____
Respect for property	Yes _____	No _____	Not sure _____

7. Do you feel the school has helped your child maintain a good feeling about himself or herself?
Yes _____ No _____ Not sure _____

8. Has your child discussed with you any of the following: school assemblies, student-to-student interaction discussions, human relations program (3–6).
Yes _____ No _____

9. Please give your comments and recommendations regarding the attitudinal aspects of the school program.

_____

_____

_____

_____

III. SCHOOL-HOME COMMUNICATION .

1. Do you feel adequately informed about school programs and policies – what goes on at school?
Yes _____ No _____

2. Do you feel welcome to visit the school?
Yes _____ No _____

3. Have you visited your child's classroom when class was in session?
Yes _____ No _____

4. If you have visited the classroom, did you find the environment helpful to learning?
Very helpful _____ Moderately helpful _____ Not very helpful _____

5. If your child has a problem at school that he or she can't resolve, does he or she know what to do or who to see?
Yes _____ No _____ Not sure _____

6. Did you have any problems this year which you pursued?
Yes _____ No _____

7. Did you feel that the person consulted was receptive?
Yes _____ No _____

8. Did a solution evolve?
Yes _____ No _____ Somewhat _____

Comments _____

_____

IV. SCHOOL PROGRAMS
We welcome your comments about the following:

	Super	OK	Poor	Don't Know	Comment
Library					
Art Alley					
Music Program					
PWT Program					
Art Docent Program (4–6)					
Tutoring Room					
Multicultural Program (K–3)					
Resource Room					
Student-to-Student Interaction Office (4–6)					
Cafeteria					
PTA					
Advisory Council (School Site Council)					
Other					

V. FUTURE PLANNING

1. If you could change one thing at this school, what would it be?

2. Do you feel this questionnaire is an effective method for evaluating our school? Please be specific in your comments.

3. Would you attend a parent education workshop on any of these topics? Please rank with numbers your priority.
   How to help my child with reading
   How to help my child with math
   How to be a more effective parent
   How to improve my child's behavior
   How to help my child become more self-directed
   How to help my child develop a positive self-image
   Stages children go through
   Learning about nutrition
   Learning about first aid and safety
   Parent effectiveness training (PET)
   Other _____

THANK YOU FOR YOUR TIME AND SUGGESTIONS – YOU MAKE A DIFFERENCE!

Signature (Optional)

FIGURE 10.6
Participation Observation Checklist

EXPERIMENT WITH PRISM AND JAR WITH WATER
LESSON: Prism—spectrum of colors in light

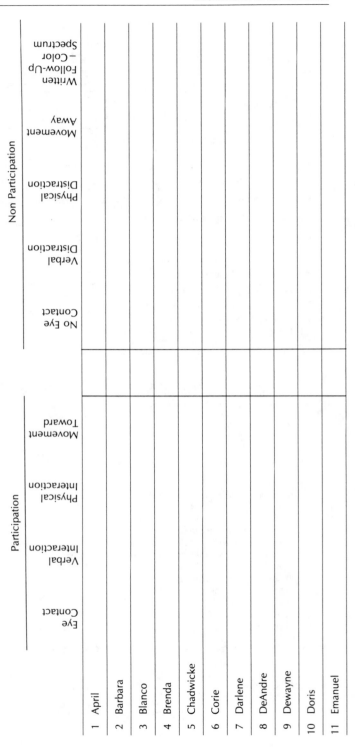

12	Felipe
13	George
14	Gerald
15	Helen
16	Jeremy
17	Jermal
18	Jorie
19	Kelly
20	Mica
21	Nefertiti
22	Niedra
23	Roderick
23	Tammy
24	Tyrone
25	Victor
26	Reginald
27	

FIGURE 10.7
Checklist for Evaluating Evaluation Instruments

Evaluation Instrument: a definition: An evaluation instrument (or test) is simply a device
for obtaining a sample of student performance to determine achievement of a particular objective or group of objectives. The test or tests must:
    a. Measure all specific objectives.

    b. Measure the specific performance called for in the objective.

    c. Be in harmony with both the objectives and the subject matter emphasized in
       the instruction (content validity).

    d. Must measure sufficiently large samples of performance to provide dependable
       and reproducible results.

    e. Measure student performance at the same taxonomic level as that specified in
       the objective (re: Bloom's taxonomy).

	YES	NO
1. Has a test or tests been devised for measuring each specific ob-jective?	_____	_____
2. Does the performance called for in the test correspond to the performance specified in the objective?	_____	_____
3. Does the test have content validity? How well do tasks of this test represent outcomes of instruction as specified in the ob-jectives?	_____	_____
4. Does the test measure a sufficiently large sample of perfor-mance to provide dependable results?	_____	_____
5. Does the test measure the objectives at the taxonomic level specified (re: Bloom's taxonomy)?	_____	_____

Comments:

From Norman E. Gronlund, *Stating Behavioral Objectives for Classroom Instruction* (London, 1978)

propriate handouts, media, and evaluation instruments are prepared.
Our appraoch is applied here in creating a "minicurriculum"
specifically for training.

    Members of the original project team now assume a new role.
They have been learners, writers, and evaluators in previous stages,
but now they become trainers. From their expertise in the develop-

FIGURE 10.8
Sample Letter to Proposed Pilot Test Participants

Dear Mr./Ms. _____ :

I have been working for the last year on a project to develop an elementary curriculum in solar energy with colleagues from the USC School of Engineering and the
Jet Propulsion Laboratories. We enlisted the help of 21 teacher experts from local
school districts to generate goals, objectives, and lesson plans. At this point, we are
ready to pilot test our materials in selected classrooms in the city, chiefly to determine if our lessons are as good as we think they are, and secondly, to be sure that
they are equally efficient with children from various social and ethnic backgrounds.
Toward this purpose, we have deliberately chosen three schools – A, B, and C – for
invited participation.

Our plan is this. We want to send our graduate project assistant to work with one
classroom teacher in each grade, K–6, in your school for two whole academic days
during September and October. Our graduate assistant will work as a team with the
regular classroom teacher in each case. Besides the two days of classroom instruction for the children, he will also be available to meet with the teacher a day
before for an hour's orientation. All together, if we work with one of your classes in
each grade, it should be possible to present our curriculum to one classroom group
of each grade level in your school within a three-week time frame. We realize that
solar energy content is new to many teachers, and for that reason we feel that it is
important to have one of our assistants available at all times.

I know that you will want to talk with your teachers about allowing us to team with
them to teach students about solar energy. Our view is that the advantages to them
might be a) to offer a special science unit to their youngsters, and b) to acquire
some personal expertise in teaching solar energy content in the future. Of course,
their cooperation will be highly valued by us, for it will mean that the Department
of Energy will disseminate the curriculum that we have prepared to other children in
the United States.

With all of the activity of closing school, I understand that it may be impossible for
you to discuss our project with your faculty. However, if you do have any idea
about their interest for September, I would much appreciate hearing from you. I will
follow up with a phone call on _____[date]_____ .

Thank you in advance for your support.

Best wishes,

_____

ment of the curriculum package, they can speak to these main
points: the method by which the curriculum was developed, the
organization of lessons, and the questions to be answered in evaluation. These team members can also field questions from the new
users, comment on the intended purpose of various parts of the curriculum, demonstrate teaching methodology, or teach skills. Most of
all, such team members become a trusted resource.

   After training, follow-up is crucial. If the project cannot provide
sufficient funding for a member of the original project team to remain
on the pilot test site, consistent support must be available through ac-

FIGURE 10.9
Sample Note to Participants in Pilot Test

MEMORANDUM

TO: Pilot test teachers

FROM:

DATE:

SUBJECT: Evaluation materials

We are delighted with your positive and constructive comments regarding the lessons you have tried with your children. In anticipating our reports to the Department of Energy, we would much appreciate your additional help with the enclosed sets of evaluation materials:

1. Brief evaluation form marked Teacher Evaluation for each lesson taught

2. 30 copies of *Student Evaluation of Solar Energy Lessons* to use *once* at end of unit

3. 30 copies of *Parent Evaluation* for use *once* at the end of the unit (We know that not all of these will be returned)

I am leaving a large envelope with _____ in the office to collect your data. We will be glad to tally your student and parent response. If your appraisals could be ready for us on _____, we would be very pleased.

Thank you again for all your work.

Cordially,

---

tual visits or through hot-line answers to telephone questions. No user of the curriculum wants to feel abandoned with the new material. Therefore, periodic meetings to answer questions and to discuss potential problems are absolutely necessary.

Just as in the various developmental stages of the curriculum design, deadlines are important for structuring work. Materials in inservice training will outline target dates, indicating that the pilot test does, indeed, have a beginning and an end. A gentle reminder of the deadline can come in a note, accompanied by requisite forms (See Figure 10.9).

When the training for pilot test is complete and data from the target classrooms are collected, the inservice training can be evaluated for its effectiveness. A self-report questionnaire (Figure 10.10) can give the project team insights into the perceived effectiveness of the training. Feedback can be used to modify the presentation for future pilot test training.

FIGURE 10.10
Individual Appraisal of Training's Effectiveness

This questionnaire is attempting to gain information about the effectiveness and relevance of the training sessions. Foremost is the concern that the time and energy committed to this project is spent constructively and meaningfully. The next 15 questions overlap in some respects, but they are all getting at the same thing: where and in what way can services to the curriculum users be improved so that training on site is easier and more effective? All information requested is for statistical/research purposes and will be kept confidential.

Example:

1. Rainy days are depressing.

   a. strongly disagree
   b. disagree
   c. neither agree nor disagree
   d. agree
   e. strongly agree

If you "agree" to this statement, fill in the answer sheet at question 1, under the letter "d." If you "strongly disagree," fill in the slot under the letter "a," then go on to the next question.

DIRECTIONS: When answering questions in this section, please think about training you have received in the curricular area. Remember to respond to each question based on the "strongly agree," "agree," "neither agree nor disagree," "disagree," or "strongly disagree" format.

_____ 1. From the beginning, it was clear what topics would be covered.

_____ 2. To have clearly understood the material presented required more time than was allotted.

_____ 3. The consultant's presentation was well-organized and clearly focused on the training subject.

_____ 4. I am prepared to train others in this content area.

_____ 5. There was too much theory and not enough practical application.

_____ 6. The presentation was organized in an effective manner.

_____ 7. I had sufficient time to familiarize myself with the material and apply it to school-related problems.

_____ 8. The consultant quickly and competently met my needs in this content area.

_____ 9. I received adequate feedback about my use of the material.

_____ 10. Less complex material was necessary in the limited training time.

_____ 11. Training in the use of the material was superficial.

_____ 12. The consultant's presentation was well prepared, and appropriate to the kind of problems faced at the school site.

_____ 13. I am motivated to train others in the content area.

_____ 14. Material presented was relevant to school-site needs.

_____ 15. Training techniques were clearly identified.

TABLE 10.3
Parent Evaluation of Solar Energy Lesson

	School A				
	Grade level		Yes		No
1. Did your son/daughter tell you that the class was studying solar energy?	K	14	70%	6	30%
		4	50%	4	50%
	1	7	70%	3	30%
	2	7	70%	3	30%
	3	9	90%	1	10%
	1–2	19	95%	1	5%
2. Did your youngster talk about conserving energy in your home?	K	15	75%		25%
		3	37.5%	5	62.5%
	1	6	60%	4	40%
	2	5	62.5%	3	37.5%
	3	6	60%	4	40%
	1–2	14	70%	6	30%

TABLE 10.4
Student Evaluation of Solar Energy Lesson

	School A						
	Grade level	Not much		OK		A lot	
1. I thought the lessons were interesting.	K	3	15%	3	15%	17	85%
		2	20%	4	40%	4	40%
	1	0	0%	2	10%	18	90%
	1–2	0	0%	3	12%	22	88%
	2	2	8%	1	4%	22	88%
	3	0	0%	3	12%	22	'88%
2. I understood the lessons on solar energy.	K	0	0%	1	5%	19	95%
		4	40%	3	30%	2	30%
	1	0	0%	0	0%	19	100%
	1–2	1	4%	3	12%	21	84%
	2	0	0%	5	20%	20	80%
	3	0	0%	6	20%	24	80%
3. I want to learn more about solar energy.	K	0	0%	0	0%	22	100%
		4	33%	5	42%	3	25%
	1	0	0⅛%	0	0%	19	100%
	1–2	3	12%	5	20%	17	69%
	2	4	16%	0	0%	21	84%
	3	1	4%	1	4%	23	92%
4. I have already told my family about solar lessons we did in class.	K	0	0%	0	0%	20	100%
		10	71%	2	14%	2	14%
	1	0	0%	0	0%	19	100%
	1–2	3	12%	5	20%	17	68%
	2	7	28%	3	12%	15	60%
	3	3	10%	7	23%	20	67%

EXAMINING TEST RESULTS

As data arrive from pilot test sites, they can be organized into meaningful tables for evaluation reports. Pilot test data from School A in the solar energy project appear in Figure 10.11 and Tables 10.3, 10.4, 10.5, 10.6.

Although still in "raw" form, the data from School A provided feedback. The teacher comments, in particular, were useful in pointing out areas where objectives could be clearer or more materials were required. The project team members could close the feedback loop by going directly back from the evaluation stage to the necessary steps for revision and modification. With each pilot test, feedback can be built into the curriculum.

EVALUATION AS AN ONGOING PROCESS

In our approach, it is through evaluation at each step that the final curriculum is developed. Evaluation is a core process in our model, essential for any change. Similarly, when the project is complete — that is, ready for dissemination after pilot test — it still has not achieved its final form. Input from users on a wide scale will provide feedback for more revisions, more modifications, and improvements over the years of its use.

FIGURE 10.11
Summary of School A Pilot Test — Solar Energy Curriculum

Table 10.3 showing results of parent evaluation of solar energy lessons, indicates in many cases (median percentage of 70%) that the child told his or her parents the class was studying solar energy. In addition, parents reported that their youngsters also talked about conserving energy at home.

Table 10.4 documents students' own reports of their reactions to the solar energy lessons. Their answers to all four questions were overwhelmingly in the "A lot" column, demonstrating positive feelings about their study of solar energy.

Table 10.5 reports cumulative data from the pilot test classrooms in School A on teacher name, grade level, lesson taught, time necessary for lesson, and learner reaction. *All* of the learner reactions were good (with some write-ins of "excellent") with the exception of three reactions of "confused."

Table 10.6 summarizes teacher recommendations. All teacher comments are aimed at concluding this statement: "In my professional opinion I feel that this lesson could be improved by _____." They express pleasure with the demonstration materials and with the quality of the lessons; they make constructive suggestions for improvement as well — e.g., "Make objective statement clearer" and "Provide materials for more activities."

TABLE 10.5
Teacher Evaluation of Solar Energy Lessons

				School A			
					Learner Reaction		
Teacher	Grade	Lesson	Time	Good	Fair	Poor
1	K	A-K- Daedalus	20 min.	Excellent		
1	K	A-1 Sun energy	20 min.	X		
1	K	B-1-I Scientific Method	10+ min.	X		
1	K	B-2-K Measurement	20 min.	X		
1	K	B-3-K Energy	17 min. cooking 20 min. teaching	Excellent		
1	K	B-4-I Renewable Energy	15–20 min.	X		
2	1	What energy is	60 min.	X		
2	1	Energy and Life	40 min.	X		
2	1	Energy Measurement	45 min.	X		
2	1	Scientific Method	60 min.	X		
2	1	Energy and How we live	90 min.	X		
2	1	Sun and light	90 min.	X		
3	1–2	2-K Sink-Float	30 min.	X		
3	1–2	2II Scientific Method	40 min.	X		
3	1–2	A-K Daedalus	60 min.	X		
3	1–2	A-1 Sun-Earth Relationship	30 min.	X		
3	1–2	A-2 Properties of Light	60 min.	X		
3	1–2	B-1-I Energy +	40 min.		Confused	
3	1–2	B-1-II Life +	over a		X	
3	1–2	2-1 Scientific Method	three-week period		X	
3	1–2	B-3-I Forms of energy	15 min.	X		
3	1–2	B-3-II Forms of Energy	45 min.	X		
3	1–2	B-2-I Energy Measurement	30 min.	X		
3	1–2	B-2-II Energy Measurement	30 min.	X		
3	1–2	B-4-II Conservation	60 min.	X		

4	2	Energy and Life	35 min.	X
4	2	Energy and the way we live	35 min.	X
4	2	Special Properties of Light	45 min.	X
4	2	The Sun Energy	45 min.	X
4	2	Energy Measurements	60 min.	X
5	3	Photo Cards	One	X
5	3	Sun of a cell	month's	X
5	3	Sun store	science	X
5	3	Solar House	lessons	X

TABLE 10.6
Teacher Recommendations, Solar Energy Lesson

In my professional opinion I feel that this lesson could be improved by:

Kindergarten Comments:
1. Story of Daedalus and Icarus.

The use of a filmstrip of the Daedalus and Icarus seemed to be a great follow-up to the oral telling of the story. The children were fascinated with the story. I was amazed when a week later we reviewed the story, most of the children (75%) were able to retell the story with amazing accuracy. Moreover, the children showed a good understanding of how the Greek myth related to ways in which the sun gives us energy.

2. The sun gives us energy; and how the earth rotates.

I eliminated the part of the lesson about the standing in the sun and shade because we have talked about the differences so often that the activity seemed redundant for this particular group of children. I read the book *The Day We Saw the Sun Come Up* which is an excellent book for explaining the rotation of the earth. Then the children used a globe and a flashlight to act out the relationship between the earth and the sun. The children's subsequent frequent references to the sun always shining in some part of the world and talk about the nighttime in China while they are here in school, all seem to be evidence of the children's comprehension or interest in these particular concepts.

3. Scientific method of study of plant growth.

The children all seemed to have a good understanding that the plant needed sun in order to grow. However, there was a wide range of hypotheses of how long it would take for the covered leaves to turn brown. (Many thought an hour or less without sun would cause the leaves to turn brown.) The range of predictions of time raised much interest in the experiment. The experiment is still going on in the classroom.

4. Concept of measurement.

Although my class had already spent a week or so studying the measurement of temperature, trying to combine so many different kinds of measurement in one lesson seems too much. Children really want to experience measurement, and I think dealing with one kind of measurement at a time would make more sense to young children.

As a class the children went on with the study of measurement. They created their own thermometer. The use of the sun-of-a-cell and the silicon cell and meter were *extremely exciting* experiences for the children. They became quite involved with this new means of measuring energy.

5. *What energy is*

The most frustrating aspect of this lesson was trying to find a sunny day to use our "10¢ hot dog cooker". However, once we found a sunny day the lesson was terrific and made quite an impression on the children.

I found a book in the public library, *Energy from the Sun* by Melvin Berger, which was of tremendous help in explaining "what is energy." It's an excellent book!

6. *Renewable and nonrenewable energy sources.*

We did not use the part of the lesson about turning the desk "on and off" (my children don't have desks). However, we used the rest of the lesson, including lighting the paper with the match, etc. We also continued the discussion on ways to save nonrenewable energy sources; and for homework the children went home to see how many ways they could conserve energy at home.

Again, I used the book *Energy from the Sun* by Melvin Berger, which was excellent enrichment for this lesson.

First Grade Comments:
7. *What energy is.*

We need additional follow-up materials.

8. *Energy and life.*

We need a film and more follow-up materials.

9. *Sun and light.*

Additional follow-up would be helpful.

First-Second Grade Comments:
10. *Sink-float.*

We really enjoyed this.

11. *Scientific method.*

Excellent way of visually presenting scientific method.

12. *Story of Daedalus and Icarus.*

Read story with some dramatization. They were interested, but a mild reaction. It seemed a little difficult for them to visualize and comprehend without pictures.

Located a tape and cassette in school.

Eye Gate Series: *Myths and Legends of Ancient Rome and Greece Dadealus and Icarus.*

The children were captivated with this. They asked many questions.

13. *Some properties of light.* (Taught by Joel)

Children still talk about this terrific lesson.

14. *Energy and life/Scientific method.*

We covered one leaf on four different house plants with aluminum foil. After 3 weeks they were wilted looking but the leaves did not turn yellow as most children had predicted. I felt the experiment was incomplete and somewhat confusing.

15. *Various forms energy can take.*

Have wanted to use solar hot dog cooker for the last few days; however, the weather has been too rainy or cloudy. Will do later.

16. *Energy measurements, Grade 2.*

Enjoyed three-color thermometer and radiometer.

17. *Ways to accomplish tasks/Energy conservation.*

A set of pictures called *Save the Dinosaurs,* from *Chevron Instructional Units* was helpful in illustrating fossil fuels energy conservation.

Second Grade Comments:
18. *Energy and life.*

Covering some leaves didn't show much results (plants were too hearty).

Objective: Children will be able to see and comprehend that plants need sun to live.

Activities: One plant out where it could get light. Other plant in the closet. After (?) duration we will make a comparison on the growth, color, and vitality of the plant. 99%.

Evaluation: Children are observing and have concluded that plants need sun light to grow and live. (Will continue to observe the isolated plant.)

19. *Energy and the way we live.*

Objective: Children be able to identify the correct sources that are reusable or renewable, and conclude that solar energy is reuseable.

Activities: Film and discussion. Pollution, transportation, bus. Discussion: What form of energy does the bus use? Do we get any pollutions? What other form of energy can you think of that may be possible? Will solar cause pollution? Can we reuse solar energy? Use activity sheet (kinds of energy).

Evaluation: Children comprehended (80%) that solar energy has many advantages because it is reusable and causes no pollution.

20. *Special properties of light.*

Simplify the objective.

Objective: Children be able to comprehend that light can bend and that it is composed of many colors.

Activities: Used a prism and a hand mirror.

Evaluation: 90% of the children were excited about the prism producing the spectrum of colors. The hand mirror showed how light can bend. Excellent and exciting lesson.

21. *The sun energy.*

Excellent: Motivation to continue other activities with the comprehension that the sun provides energy for the use of man and to make progress in another form of energy to its maximum.

Objective: After listening and seeing a film strip of Daedalus and Icarus, children should be able to comprehend that the sun provides energy.

22. *Energy measurements.*

Because of bad weather, was not able to accomplish this task. However, will continue this when the sun is out and smiling.

Third Grade Comments:
I cannot evaluate the lessons individually because I handled the material differently. We were already studying energy at the time. The children built solar houses and measured the amount of energy with equipment from you.

At a final meeting of the original development team, the members will wish to evaluate their own experiences. Despite a well-earned sense of accomplishment, they will identify places where they would divide their team work differently or make different types of decisions, a natural aspect of a cohesive working group. Each time curriculum is designed, more is learned about the process of curriculum development that may be applied to the next curriculum effort.

For those committed to an evaluation for every task, we encourage the use or adaptation of the Curriculum Development Checklist (Figure 10.12) prepared by the California Curriculum Alliance for project teams for overall appraisal of their own work.

Although Principle 1 of the checklist is assumed to have been fulfilled at the beginning of curriculum development, work toward the other thirteen principles can be examined by the members. Again, issues that need attention are identified, and modifications are inserted at the appropriate levels.

SUMMARY

This chapter has addressed the necessity for evaluation and for designing an evaluation plan, and has defined formative and summative processes. Models of evaluation were identified, but project teams were encouraged to generate their own appraisal strategies as part of this approach to curriculum design. Several brief evaluation forms were included as examples, and sampling problems were discussed. Training users for pilot test requires the project team to plan a "minicurriculum" for inservice training. Examples of pilot test data from the solar energy project were included. Finally, the project team was encouraged to apply its evaluative standards to its own work on the curriculum they had designed.

FOLLOW-UP ACTIVITIES

1. Identify three fundamental questions you need to answer about the curriculum materials you have produced.
2. Make a plan for going about the evaluation of those three questions.
3. Write a sample letter seeking volunteers to help pilot test your materials.
4. Collect data, using instruments you have prepared for the pilot test.
5. Write a brief report on your findings from the pilot test.
6. Explain the differences between formative and summative evaluation.
7. Discuss four hazards in using results of summative evaluation.
8. Explain why sampling techniques are important.
9. Outline plans for training of pilot test participants.
10. Prepare an evaluation instrument for use in a pilot test.

FIGURE 10.12
Curriculum Development Checklist

Curriculum development is a human interaction process through which curriculum decisions are made. Curriculum decision makers are encouraged to use this checklist in discussing and assessing curriculum needs and programs. Fourteen curriculum development principles are identified in the checklist. Each principle is followed by questions designed to help determine to what extent the principle is being used. A "0" rating of the principle would indicate no use; a "5" rating would indicate full use. The questions are illustrative and are intended to generate additional questions and discussion.

Principle
1. Curriculum development is based on the philosophical beliefs of the community, as determined within the context of societal needs.
   a. Does the local Board of Education have an identified policy giving direction to curriculum development?
   b. Is the community involved in the development of the district philosophy and goals?
   c. Do the goals reflect societal needs?
   d. Are the goals realistic for the student population? (e.g., Is the number of college prep courses proportionate to the number of students actually going on to college?)

To what extent is this principle being used?   No use____ ____ ____ ____Full use
                                                      0   1   2   3   4   5

2. Curriculum development accommodates student differences and is based upon knowledge of learner growth and development.
   a. Do objectives reflect the emotional, social, and intellectual developmental stages of the learner?
   b. Is diagnosis of student needs used to determine placement of children? (e.g., Are student interests and reading levels used to determine reading activities?)

To what extent is this principle being used?   No use____ ____ ____ ____Full use
                                                      0   1   2   3   4   5

3. Principles of learning are critical to planning teaching and learning activities.
   a. Is the need for repetition made clear in those teaching/learning activities that require repeated practice?
   b. Do learning activities progress from lower to higher levels of thinking?

To what extent is this principle being used?   No use____ ____ ____ ____Full use
                                                      0   1   2   3   4   5

4. The curriculum development process is based on a cycle of planning-implementation-evaluation.
   a. Is there a clearly defined, systematic curriculum development process for the district?
   b. Is the curriculum development plan compatible with the state schedule for Frameworks and text materials adoption?
   c. Is adequate planning time built into the schedule?
   d. Is staff development an integral part of implementation plans?
   e. Is evaluation information used in setting goals and objectives?

To what extent is this principle being used?   No use____ ____ ____ ____Full use
                                                      0   1   2   3   4   5

5. Teaching methods and materials reflect existing and developing learning modes (visual, auditory, tactile, intuitive) of each student, consistent with learning objectives.
   a. Is the program planned in terms of both strong and weak learning modes of each student) (e.g., Is the auditorily oriented student given opportunities to use tape recordings to reinforce skills?)
   b. Are opportunities given for students to use cognitive and affective learning skills in a wide variety of learning activities?
   c. Is a variety of materials available for cognitive and affective learning?

   To what extent is this principle being used?

No use					Full use
0	1	2	3	4	5

6. Determination of scope and sequence is important in curriculum planning.
   a. Are the major learnings defined for each area of the curriculum?
   b. Is the sequence of learning activities geared to the major developmental stages of each learner?

   To what extent is this principle being used?

No use					Full use
0	1	2	3	4	5

7. Optimal progress of learners requires articulated planning by staff.
   a. Does a district plan exist that ensures articulation between age levels and subject matter in all areas of the curriculum?
   b. Does staff work together to articulate the educational program?
   c. Are there methods and records that help teachers keep track of student progress?

   To what extent is this principle being used?

No use					Full use
0	1	2	3	4	5

8. Curriculum content is relevant to the learner and is significant to society.
   a. Does the learner take part in content and activity planning?
   b. Are major societal concerns of the past, present, and future utilized to motivate the student?

   To what extent is this principle being used?

No use					Full use
0	1	2	3	4	5

9. Instructional materials are selected to fit the curriculum, not vice versa.
   a. Does curriculum planning and evaluation precede the selection of instructional materials?
   b. Do teachers and others involved in curriculum planning participate in selecting materials?

   To what extent is this principle being used?

No use					Full use
0	1	2	3	4	5

10. A comprehensive, balanced curriculum is developed.
    a. Is instructional time allocated to all curriculum areas (e.g., social studies, science, art, music)?
    b. Are basic skills taught in all content areas?

    To what extent is this principle being used?

No use					Full use
0	1	2	3	4	5

11. Curriculum planning includes provisions to meet related staff development needs.
    a. Are staff developmet programs provided to implement legislated changes?
    b. Are teachers involved in assessing needs and in making decisions regarding staff development?

To what extent is this principle being used?

No use ___ ___ ___ ___ Full use
  0   1   2   3   4   5

12. In the process of curriculum development, appropriate human and material resources are identified and used.
    a. Are the State Curriculum Frameworks and the County Course of Study used as resources?
    b. Are teachers involved in the curriculum development process, and do they serve as resources for other teachers?
    c. Are sample materials available for teachers to study and review?

To what extent is this principle being used?

No use ___ ___ ___ ___ Full use
  0   1   2   3   4   5

13. Consideration is given to the integration of subject matter areas.
    a. Are time and resources set aside to plan for curriculum integration?
    b. Are programs and instructional materials available as resources?

To what extent is this principle being used?

No use ___ ___ ___ ___ Full use
  0   1   2   3   4   5

14. Curriculum development reflects an openness to new and changing ideas.
    a. Are opportunities given to teachers to research, suggest, and try new ideas and materials?
    b. Are programs being considered for adoption or adaptation carefully evaluated?

To what extent is this principle being used?

No use ___ ___ ___ ___ Full use
  0   1   2   3   4   5

REFERENCES

Campbell, D. T., & Stanley, J. *Experimental and Quasi-Experimental Designs for Research.* Chicago: R. McNally, 1963.

Cronbach, I. "Course Improvement Through Evaluation." *Teachers Record* 4 (1963): 672–83.

Gottman, J., & Clasen, R. *Evaluation in Education: A Practitioner's Guide.* Ithaca, Ill.: F. E. Peacock Publishers, 1972.

Gronlund, N. E. *Stating Behavioral Objectives for Classroom Instruction.* 2d ed. London: Macmillan, 1978.

Horst, D., et al. *A Practical Guide to Measuring Project Impact on Student Achievement.* Monograph Series on Education No. 1. Washington, D.C.: U.S. Office of Education, 1975.

Isaac, S. & Michael, W. *Handbook in Research and Evaluation.* San Diego: EdITS Publishers, 1977.

Krop, L., "Evaluating the Effectiveness of a Modern Systems Approach to Field Instruction in Graduate School Work Education." Bethesda, Maryland: ERIC ED 104305, 1973.

SOLAR ENERGY CURRICULUM

Appendix A contains an example of a curriculum designed according to our approach. It is a model for other curriculum developers. Our approach to curriculum design was the method used in developing A Solar Energy Curriculum for Elementary Schools,* a project funded by the United States Department of Energy since 1977. Beginning with the Introduction to Curriculum, the materials briefly sampled here show how one lesson, "B_1," emerges from Block B, "Energy and Life," in the Structure of the Discipline (Figure A.3), and then from Goal BI (Table A.1). The specific behavioral objective was: "The first-grade learner demonstrates a knowledge that sunlight is essential to all plant life, through making a pictographic and written word record of the condition of a plant's leaves when covered or uncovered." One of the materials created by the project team, the record sheet to confirm student performance, is included with the lesson. In pilot tests, as reported in Tables 10.3, 10.4, 10.5, and 10.6, this lesson was effective. One of the teacher's comments in formative evaluation was:

> The children all seemed to have a good understanding that the plant needed sun in order to grow. However, there was a wide range of hypotheses of how long it would take for the covered leaves to turn brown. (Many thought an hour or less without sun would cause the leaves to turn brown.) The range of predictions of time raised much interest in the experiment. The experiment is still going on in the classroom.

---

*Lampert, Seymour; Kathleen M. Wulf; & Gilbert Yanow. *A Solar Energy Curriculum for Elementary Schools.* Washington, D.C.: United States Department of Energy, 1979.

INTRODUCTION TO CURRICULUM

In view of accelerated depletion of "conventional" energy sources, there is a need to educate our society in the use and conservation of these dwindling reserves. Not only will our present lifestyles be affected but also those of future generations. Therefore, there is a concomitant need for development and implementation of alternative energy sources, primarily of solar energy.

Since students now in elementary schools will be the sector of the world's population most directly affected by problems of energy depletion, it is appropriate immediately to provide them with programs dealing with concepts of solar energy. This project, then, aims to educate children in grades K–6 toward two major goals: an appreciation of the need for energy conservation and an understanding of the potential of the sun as a suitable alternative energy resource.

The lessons, demonstration experiments, and evaluation strategies for this program in solar energy were developed using a systematic model for curriculum design. An interdisciplinary team of teachers and subject matter specialists shared expertise at appropriate points in the process. All participants worked within the following plan (Figures A.1, A.2):

1. Selecting the content of a solar energy curriculum.
2. Writing goals for learners.
3. Turning goals into instructional objectives.
4. Generating appropriate lessons.
5. Deciding upon evaluation.

Selecting the content of a solar energy curriculum. Since there were no established cohesive elementary school curricular pieces for concepts of solar energy, the development team had no fixed model of exactly which content areas were to be included. While some existing science materials addressed the energy crisis in part, none moved directly from that point into the need for solar energy. It was necessary, therefore, to create a conceptual model of solar energy, incorporating essentially a content map of what the lessons would include. This model describes both the necessary background understandings (i.e., the requisite areas of the sun and of energy), the basic content areas, and some of the related socioeconomic issues (Figure A.3).

Using the model or content map, the subject matter experts trained the educational curriculum and teacher experts in fundamental ideas of solar energy. They presented a history of the use of the sun as an energy source, early solar devices, and possibilities for future use. With such a background, the team was ready for the next step in the process: establishing goals.

FIGURE A.1
Development Process

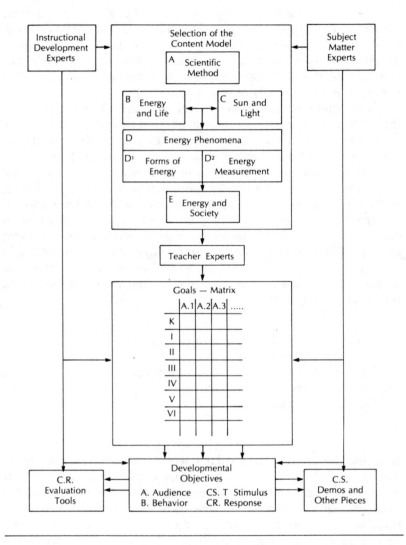

FIGURE A.2
Development Process Part II

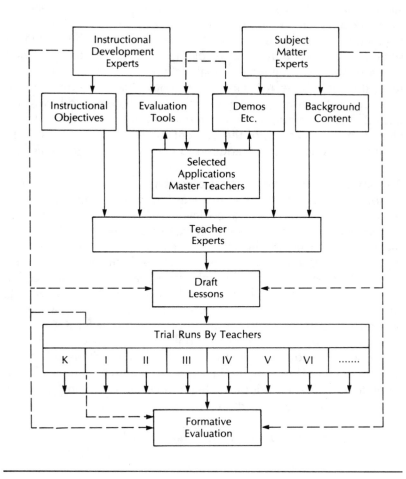

Writing goals for students.   Unlike the previous task of creating a structure, goal writing was not new to the education experts. The subject matter experts received training in proper stating of goals using work of Bloom (1956), Gronlund (1972), and Mager (1967). Basing their work on the assumption that the selection of the content of solar energy was representative of the concepts students needed to learn, the team generated goal statements from each category (e.g., the sun). Table A.1 (Goal Statements) illustrates how the process reflects the concept category, marked by letters, and how goals from that category are labeled in numerical order. Category "A," included in the selection of the content model, emerged as an "enabling goal," one that was required to help achieve other goals.

Turning goals into instructional objectives.   After goals had been established, a development matrix was formed showing goals by letter and number for each grade level (Figure A.4). Teachers, curriculum experts, and subject matter experts worked in writing teams, tackling objectives on the matrix in clusters; e.g., one team was assigned responsibility for all "A" objectives from all categories for one grade level. Continuity through grades was thereby enhanced. It will be noted that the coding used indicates Objectives A through E; the first subscript refers to the appropriate subcategory, while the second subscript refers to the appropriate grade level K–6. As the lessons were tested at various schools in Southern California, the ordering of the goals/objectives was revised to reflect these findings. The "Selection of the Content" in Figure A.3 shows the principal areas for which the lessons are presented and coded accordingly. A four-part format for objectives was employed (Figure A.5):

A   Audience: The students (grade, age, entry level).
B   Behavior (identifies, comprehends, applies, analyzes, synthesizes, evaluates).
C_S Conditions of the stimulus (after watching, reading, participating).
C_R Conditions of the response.

Generating appropriate lessons.   Again writing in teams, the workers designed lessons to facilitate growth toward meeting the objectives defined above. With the four-part statement of the objective available, writing lessons became a task of simply "fleshing out" or "building upon" the basic statement. Frequently it meant developing a worksheet or a response device for the learners. Lessons retain their code letters for category of content and numbers for independent lessons in that area.

Deciding upon evaluation.   The culmination of this systems approach to curriculum development was to provide the teacher some assessment tools. Consequently each lesson recommends an ap-

TABLE A.1
Goal Statements

A	1.	Students grow in their ability to apply the scientific method.

B	1.	The students understand that the sun is essential to all life on earth.
	2.	The students learn the physical properties of the sun.
	3.	The students learn the astronomical relationships of the sun to the earth.
	4.	The students learn that all of our sources of energy on earth are traceable to the sun.

C	1.	The students learn to recognize various forms of energy.
	2.	The students evolve a concept of "energy."
	3.	The students understand the difference between renewable and nonrenewable energy sources. (Clean/renewable is desirable and environmentally sound.)
	4.	The students learn about energy measurements.
	5.	The students understand how the present "energy crisis" is a crisis in the way we use energy.
	6.	The students know about alternative energy sources.
	7.	The students understand energy conservation.

D	1.	The students understand the basic problems involved in utilizing solar energy.
	2.	The students learn some of the ways of using solar energy. (Passive/Active-Direct/Indirect) (Matrix)
	3.	The students understand some of the technical problems involved in utilizing solar energy: collection (and noncollection-passive), conversion, utilization, storage.

E	1.	The students will be able to recognize how political issues affect solar energy technology.
	2.	The students will understand how economic issues affect solar energy.
	3.	The students will understand the environmental impact of solar energy.
	4.	The students will understand the sociological constraints on using solar energy.
	5.	The students will understand the institutional constraints on using solar energy.

propriate criterion-referenced evaluation phase. For young students in early grades, care has been taken to provide evaluation schemes which are not predicated upon the ability to read; e.g., indicate by coloring a worksheet (in the lesson) that the student has "read" a thermometer correctly. Similarly, these lessons allow for continuous progress. For example, if a kindergarten class masters all of the "C" (energy) lessons for kindergarten level, they can move directly to the first-grade lessons in Category "C" for greater depth. Grade-level labels are not intended to be restrictive.

Teachers using these curricular pieces, therefore, can be assured that they were developed systematically by an interdisciplinary team. We encourage the creative teacher to use our lessons, our teacher concept write-ups, and our demonstration devices to go beyond what we have already produced for this short course in solar energy. At this point there are possibilities for adapting more lessons from

FIGURE A.3
Selection of the Content of the Curriculum

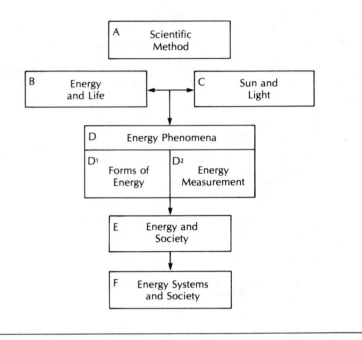

these basic ones, providing more instructional activities, and "customizing" these lessons for use with special students. It is our hope that 1) we will help you and your students achieve your goal of a deeper understanding of solar energy and that 2) you will share your critical ideas and recommendations with us.

Since we value teachers' comments concerning the lessons used with students, three short forms are included for your evaluations. We will be grateful to you if you will share your ideas with us. We will apply any useful suggestions to the final version of the curriculum.

ENERGY AND LIFE:
Unit B₁ (Approximate Grade Level 1)

Overview

This lesson allows the students to apply the scientific method to an experiment which demonstrates how the sun is essential to green plant growth. The class will fill out "lab reports" on an experiment in which one leaf of a green plant is covered with aluminum foil to prevent its receiving sunlight. Through a combination of words and pic-

FIGURE A.4
Development Matrix-Goal Statement for Each Grade Level

Goal / Grade	A	B	C	D		E
K	A_K	B_K	C_K	$(D_1)_K$	$(D_2)_K$	
I	A_I	B_I	C_I	$(D_1)_I$	(D	
II	A_{II}	B_{II}	C_{II}	$(D_1)_{II}$		
III	A_{III}	B_{III}	C_{III}			
IV	A_{IV}	B_{IV}	C_{IV}			
V	A_V	B_V	C_V			
VI	A_{VI}	B_{VI}	C_{VI}			

tures, each student will record his or her predictions, observations, and conclusions (Figure A.6).

Learning Objective

First-grade students will demonstrate a knowledge that the sun is essential to plant life through participation in a plant leaf experiment; it will be observed through their completion of a "lab report."

Evaluation

As we have noted in lesson A_I, this lesson serves as the completion of two objectives: mastery of the scientific method and knowledge that the sun is essential for green plant growth. Both of these objectives will be evaluated through the lab report worksheet. To meet objective A_I, the conclusion statement must be: "Plants need sunlight."

Special Materials

- 1 green plant
- Aluminum foil
- Lab report worksheets

FIGURE A.5
Development Objectives

A	Audience	(Who)
B	Behavior	(Learns to do What)
C_S	Conditions of the Stimulus	(Processing with What)
C_R	Conditions of the Response	(Demonstrated by Doing)

Vocabulary

• Scientist, predict, observe, experiment, conclude

Extension Exercises

• The class could see how plants grow under colored light by putting colored cellophane over the end of a cardboard box and growing the plant in the box.

LESSON PLAN

1. The class is asked, "What do you think will happen if a plant doesn't get sunlight?"
2. Review the scientific method. (GUESSING/WATCHING/DECIDING)
3. How would a scientist decide if our guess about the plant needing sunlight is correct? The scientist would set up an experiment.
4. Pass out the lab report worksheets (Figure A.6) and define the experiment:
   a. We will cover several of the leaves on this plant with aluminum foil so that they can get no sunlight.
   b. We will need to watch it every day for awhile. (It may take up to two weeks before you have significant results.)
   c. We will need to make records of the results.
5. Record the experiment on the worksheets.
6. Observe the plant daily.
7. When you think you have significant results, record the conclusions.

FIGURE A.6
Lab Report Worksheet

RECORD SHEET

NAME _____

1. THE PROBLEM _____

_____

_____

2. YOUR PREDICTION (YOUR GUESS) _____

3. OBSERVATION (WHAT HAPPENED) _____

4. ARE SQUARES 2 AND 3 THE SAME? _____

_____

COGNITIVE, AFFECTIVE, AND PSYCHOMOTOR DOMAINS

Appendix B contains the taxonomy of educational objectives for the cognitive, affective, and psychomotor domains, which is useful in preparing instructional objectives.

Cognitive Domain

Taxonomy Classification	KEY WORDS	
	Examples of Infinitives	Examples of Direct Objects
1.00 Knowledge		
1.10 Knowledge of Specifics		
1.11 Knowledge of Terminology	to define, to distinguish, to acquire, to identify, to recall, to recognize	vocabulary terms, terminology, meaning(s), definitions, referents, elements
1.12 Knowledge of Specific Facts	to recall, to recognize, to acquire, to identify	facts, factual information, (sources), (names), (dates), (events), (persons), (places), (time periods), properties, examples, phenomena
1.20 Knowledge of Ways and Means of Dealing with Specifics		
1.21 Knowledge of Conventions	to recall, to identify, to recognize, to acquire	form(s), conventions, uses, usage, rules, ways, devices, symbols, representations, style(s), format(s)

Taxonomy Classification	KEY WORDS	
	Examples of Infinitives	Examples of Direct Objects
1.22 Knowledge of Trends, Sequences	to recall, to recognize, to acquire, to identify	action(s) processes, movement(s), continuity, development(s), trend(s), sequence(s), causes, relationship(s), forces, influences
1.23 Knowledge of Classifications and Categories	to recall, to recognize, to acquire, to identify	area(s), type(s), feature(s), class(es), set(s), division(s), arrangement(s), classification(s), category/categories
1.24 Knowledge of Criteria	to recall, to recognize, to acquire, to identify	criteria, basics, elements
1.25 Knowledge of Methodology	to recall, to recognize, to acquire, to identify	methods, techniques, approaches, uses, procedures, treatments
1.30 Knowledge of the Universals and Abstractions in a Field		
1.31 Knowledge of Principles, Generalizations	to recall, to recognize, to acquire, to identify	principle(s), generalization(s), proposition(s), fundamentals, laws, principal elements, implication(s)
1.32 Knowledge of Theories and Structures	to recall, to recognize, to acquire, to identify	theories bases, interrelations, structure(s), organization(s), formulation(s)
2.00 Comprehension		
2.10 Translation	to translate, to transform, to give in own words, to illustrate, to prepare, to read, to represent, to change, to rephrase, to restate	meaning(s), sample(s), definitions, abstractions, representations, words, phrases
2.20 Interpretation	to interpret, to reorder, to rearrange, to differentiate, to distinguish, to make, to draw, to explain, to demonstrate	relevancies, relationships, essentials, aspects, new view(s), qualifications, conclusions, methods, theories, abstractions
2.30 Extrapolation	to estimate, to infer, to conclude, to predict, to differentiate, to determine, to extend, to interpolate, to extrapolate, to fill in, to draw	consequences, implications, conclusions, factors, ramifications, meanings, corollaries, effects, probabilities
3.00 Application	to apply, to generalize, to relate, to choose, to develop, to organize, to use, to employ, to transfer, to restructure, to classify	principles, laws, conclusions, effects, methods, theories, abstractions, situations, generalizations, processes, phenomena, procedures

| | KEY WORDS | |
Taxonomy Classification	Examples of Infinitives	Examples of Direct Objects
4.00 Analysis		
4.10 Analysis of Elements	to distinguish, to detect, to identify, to classify, to discriminate, to recognize, to categorize, to deduce	elements, hypothesis/ hypotheses, conclusions, assumptions, statements (of fact), statements (of intent), arguments, particulars
4.20 Analysis of Relationships	to analyze, to contrast, to compare, to distinguish, to deduce	relationships, interrelations, relevance, relevancies, themes, evidence, fallacies, arguments, cause-effect(s), consistency/ consistencies, parts, ideas, assumptions
4.30 Analysis of Organizational Principles	to analyze, to distinguish, to detect, to deduce	form(s), pattern(s), purpose(s), point(s) of view(s), techniques, bias(es), structure(s), theme(s), arrangement(s), organization(s)
5.00 Synthesis		
5.10 Production of a Unique Communication	to write, to tell, to relate, to produce, to constitute, to transmit, to originate, to modify, to document	structure(s), pattern(s), product(s), performance(s), design(s), work(s), communications, effort(s), specifics, composition(s)
5.20 Production of a Plan, or Proposed Set of Operations	to propose, to plan, to produce, to design, to specify	plan(s), objectives specification(s), schematic(s), operations, way(s), solution(s), means
5.30 Derivation of a Set of Abstract Relations	to produce, to derive, to develop, to combine, to organize, to synthesize, to classify, to deduce, to develop, to formulate, to modify	phenomena, taxonomies, concept(s), scheme(s), theories, relationships, abstractions, generalizations, hypothesis/hypotheses, perceptions, ways, discoveries
6.00 Evaluation		
6.10 Judgments in Terms of Internal Evidence	to judge, to argue, to validate, to assess, to decide	accuracy/accuracies, consistency/consistencies, fallacies, reliability, flaws, errors, precision, exactness
6.20 Judgments in Terms of External Criteria	to judge, to argue, to consider, to compare, to contrast, to standardize, to appraise	ends, means efficiency, economy/economies, utility, alternatives, courses of action, standards, theories, generalizations

From Newton S. Metfessel, William B. Michael, & Donald A. Kirsner, "Instrumentation of Bloom's and Krathwohl's Taxonomies for the Writing of Educational Objectives," *Psychology in the Schools,* 6 (July 1969): 227–31.

Affective Domain

		KEY WORDS	
Taxonomy Classification		Examples of Infinitives	Examples of Direct Objects
1.0	Receiving		
1.1	Awareness	to differentiate, to separate, to set apart, to share	sights, sounds, events, designs, arrangements
1.2	Willingness to	to accumulate, to select, to combine, to accept	models, examples, shapes, sizes, meters, cadences
1.3	Controlled or Selected Attention	to select, to posturally respond to, to listen (for), to control	alternatives, answers, rhythms, nuances
2.0	Responding		
2.1	Acquiescence in Responding	to comply (with), to follow, to commend, to approve	directions, instructions, laws, policies, demonstrations
2.2	Willingness to Respond	to volunteer, to discuss, to practice, to play	instruments, games, dramatic works, charades, burlesques
2.3	Satisfaction in Response	to applaud, to acclaim, to spend leisure time in, to augment	speeches, plays, presentations, writings
3.0	Valuing		
3.1	Acceptance of a Value	to increase measured proficiency in, to increase numbers of, to relinquish, to specify	group membership(s), artistic production(s), musical productions, personal friendships
3.2	Preference for a Value	to assist, to subsidize, to help, to support	artists, projects, viewpoints, arguments
3.3	Commitment	to deny, to protest, to debate, to argue	deceptions, irrelevancies, abdications, irrationalities
4.0	Organization		
4.1	Conceptualization of a Value	to discuss, to theorize (on), to abstract, to compare	parameters, codes, standards, goals
4.2	Organization of a Value System	to balance, to organize, to define, to formulate	systems approaches, criteria, limits
5.0	Characterization by Value of Value Complex		
5.1	Generalized Set	to revise, to change, to complete, to require	plans, behavior, methods, effort(s)
5.2	Characterization	to be rated high by peers in, to be rated high by superiors in, to be rated high by subordinates in and	humanitarianism, ethics, integrity, maturity
		to avoid, to manage, to resolve, to resist	extravagance(s), excesses, conflicts, exorbitancy/exorbitancies

From Newton S. Metfessel, William B., Michael, & Donald A. Kirsner, "Instrumentation of Bloom's and Krathwohl's Taxonomies for the Writing of Educational Objectives," *Psychology in the Schools*, 6 (July 1969): 227–31.

Psychomotor Domain

Taxonomy Classification

1.0   Reflex movements

2.0   Basic-fundamental movements

    2.1   Locomotor movements
    2.2   Nonlocomotor movements
    2.3   Manipulative movements

3.0   Perceptual abilities

    3.1   Kinesthetic discrimination
    3.2   Visual discrimination
    3.3   Auditory discrimination
    3.4   Tactile discrimination
    3.5   Coordinated perceptual abilities

4.0   Physical abilities

    4.1   Endurance
    4.2   Strength
    4.3   Flexibility
    4.4   Agility

5.0   Skilled movements

    5.1   Simple adaptive skill
    5.2   Compound adaptive skill
    5.3   Complex adaptive skill

6.0   Nondiscursive communication

    6.1   Expressive movement
    6.2   Interpretive movement

From Anita Harrow, *A Taxonomy of the Psychomotor Domain* (New York: David McKay, 1972).

MODEL LESSON FOR CRITICAL THINKING

Appendix C presents an example of a lesson from a curriculum to promote critical thinking. In the procedure, specific instructional objectives are cited. Appropriate motivational materials designed by the project team are also included.

Critical Thinking Processes

MODEL LESSON FOR MIDDLE GRADES

OBJECTIVE
Recognition of conflicting oral or written observation statements.

PERFORMANCE OBJECTIVE
Given two written advertisements of transportation to the West Coast in 1851, the learner cites the conflicting statements.

MATERIALS:

Descriptive paragraph for motivational purpose (See Figure C.1)
Copies of advertisements (See Figures C.2, C.3) for each learner, or room posters
Globe of the world
Maps of North and South America
Books as listed in the Bibliography
Charts (See Figures C.4, C.5, C.6)

CLASSROOM ORGANIZATION:

The learners are grouped for discussion, either in a circle or at desks which are facing in such a way that each learner can easily participate. Research centers should be set aside in order that different aspects of the research may take place. The learners should be able to move to the research centers to study geography, ships, covered wagons, and weather.

MOTIVATION:

1. Read to class the motivation paragraph. (See Figure C.1)
2. Teacher shows learners two posters that advertise travel to California by ship and by covered wagon. (See Figures C.2, C.3)
3. Teacher invites learners to read poster on sea trip.
4. Teacher invites learners to read poster on overland route.

PROCEDURE:

> THE LEARNER IDENTIFIES SPECIFIC DETAILS THAT DIFFER IN THE TWO VERSIONS.

1. Teacher asks learners to identify the details that differ and those that claim to be similar.
   a. Differences may be:
      1. Land vs. water journeys
      2. Price
      3. Departure dates
      4. Dangers
   b. The similarity is that both make claims to be safest, fastest, most comfortable way to travel to California.

> THE LEARNER DISTINGUISHES CRUCIAL FROM NONCRUCIAL DIFFERENCES THAT HAVE BEEN IDENTIFIED.

2. The teacher will chart the learners' responses on Chart 1 (see Figure C.4).
3. The teacher asks the learners to decide whether both advertisements making similar statements will probably be true and whether the differences are really important.
   Possible responses might be:
   a. Yes, they are true.
   b. No, they are probably both the same.
   c. The differences would be important because the advertisements cause you to decide how to go.
   d. There were no agencies to control advertisements in those days.

> THE LEARNER RAISES QUESTIONS AS TO REASONS FOR DIF-FERENCES.

4. The teacher asks the learners to discuss why each advertisement can make similar claims.
   Possible responses might be:
   a. Desire to sell more tickets and therefore make a profit.
   b. Desire to have people come to California to increase the population and commerce.
   c. Desire to sell mining equipment and other provisions.
   d. Desire of owners to have others use their form of transportation and therefore make more money.

FIGURE C.1
Paragraph Read to the Class for Motivation

It is 1851. A man from New York hears about the discovery of gold in California and the
great wealth to be gained there. He decides to go to California. In gaining information
on how to travel, he reads advertisements on the overland route. The overland route
pictures the route to be one of travel by covered wagon. The other route is by ship from
New York by way of Cape Horn to San Francisco.

FIGURE C.2

FIGURE C.3

FIGURE C.4
Chart 1

SEA VOYAGE	LAND JOURNEY
Differences	Similarities
Differences	Similarities

THE LEARNER RECOGNIZES POSSIBILITY OF BIAS.

5. The teacher asks the learners if there is a possibility that the writers of these advertisements could be partial to their means of transportation.
    Possible response might be:
    "The writers work for the individual companies and therefore try to make their company appear to be the best."

THE LEARNER RECOGNIZES THE POSSIBILITY OF OPINION OR INTERPRETATION VS. FACT.

6. The teacher asks the learners to identify any part of the advertisements that might be an opinion.
7. The teacher will list the responses in the appropriate column on Chart 2 (See Figure C.5).

THE LEARNER RECOGNIZES THAT INFORMATION WAS INTENTIONALLY OR UNINTENTIONALLY OMITTED.

8. The teacher asks the learners if they feel that a potential traveler should have more information about either trip before making a decision. "What do you suppose the advertisements did *not* say? Why?"
    Possible responses might be:
    a. The learner will desire more information about the weather.
    b   None of the hardships is mentioned, and therefore more information is needed.
    c. A firm travel time is not given.

FIGURE C.5
Chart 2

List in the proper section the portions of the advertisements that are facts and those parts that are opinion.	
SEA VOYAGE	
Fact	Opinion
LAND JOURNEY	
Fact	Opinion

9. The teacher asks the learners to speculate as to why some things were not mentioned.

> THE LEARNER COMPARES DATA GIVEN WITH DATA FROM PERSONAL EXPERIENCE.

10. The teacher asks the learner to recount experiences of sea trips or horse-drawn vehicles.
    Possible responses might be:
    a. The learners respond with various experiences that are comparable.
    b. The learners compare their experiences with what they think they might encounter in an actual journey.

> THE LEARNER RECOGNIZES WHEN MORE DATA IS NEEDED TO ESTABLISH REASONS FOR DIFFERENCES.

11. The teacher asks the learners what other information they need to compare the advertising with the actual trip.
    Possible responses might be:
    a. The learners state that they need more information about the conditions of both journeys.
    b. The learners may state that modern experiences do not quite compare with the conditions when these trips were being taken.

> THE LEARNER RECOGNIZES THE SOURCES OF ADDITIONAL DATA (RESOURCE PERSONS, VARIOUS MEDIA, REFERENCE MATERIALS, ETC.)

12. The teacher poses the question, "Where do you think we can find more information about these two routes?"
13. The learners list with the teacher all sources of information.
14. The teacher directs the learners to additional sources of data in the reference center.

(The learners refer to books, maps, and globes to chart simulated journeys by land and sea.)

> THE LEARNER RECOGNIZES THAT SOME SOURCES ARE MORE RELIABLE FOR CERTAIN PURPOSES THAN OTHERS.

15.   The teacher sets aside a time for the learners to do research on various data in the classroom center and school library. Materials are gathered and evaluated. (Value of sources is discussed.)

> THE LEARNER SELECTS AND RECORDS DATA RELEVANT TO THE CONFLICT.

16.   The teacher provides a chart for the learners to record data on each journey side by side: Chart 3 (See Figure C.6).
17.   The learners dramatize (e.g., through role playing) a situation similar to the sea trip or the land journey by using the knowledge gained in research to bring out the important facts of the conflict.
18.   The learners discuss the outcomes of the simulation activity.

> THE LEARNER WEIGHS THE EVIDENCE AND REACHES A DECISION AS TO WHETHER THE CONFLICT CAN BE RESOLVED.

19.   The learners may conclude that there are certain advantages with each route as well as disadvantages.
20.   The learners may conclude that neither advertisement gave a realistic account of the actual journey.

FIGURE C.6
Chart 3

DATA CHART List all the information you can find to compare the two means of travel to San Francisco.		
FACTORS	BY SEA	BY LAND
1. Departure date		
2. Length of journey		
3. Distance of journey		
4. Arrival date		
5. Expected weather		
6. Availability of food and water		
7. Availability of any outside assistance		
8. Obvious dangers		
9. Advantages		
10. Other		

21.   The learners may conclude that either method of travel might be acceptable under differing circumstances.
22.   The learners may conclude that settlers and miners were out of their minds to attempt such a trip.

BIBLIOGRAPHY:

American Heritage. *The California Gold Rush.* New York: American Heritage, 1961.

Bauer, Helen. *California Gold Days.* Sacramento: California State Department of Education, 1957.

Caughey, John. *California's Own History.* Sacramento: California State Department of Education, 1965.

Coit, Margaret. *The Westward Sweep* Vols. 4 & 5. New York: Time-Life, 1963.

Davis, Dutton. *A California Portfolio.* Los Angeles: Automobile Club of Southern California, 1970.

Lavender, David. *The Story of California.* Sacramento: California State Department of Education, 1970.

Roaring Camp. Simulation Game—Simile II. La Jolla, Calif.: Western Behavioral Sciences Institute, 1969.

Shaftel, George, et al. *Westward the Nation.* Sacramento: California State Department of Education, 1967.

Shapiro, Irwin. *The Golden Book of California.* New York: Golden Press, 1961.

Williams, Mabel. *California: A History.* Sacramento: California State Department of Education, 1965.

AN INSTRUMENT FOR THE ASSESSMENT OF INSTRUCTIONAL MATERIAL

Appendix D contains an instrument for the assessment of instructional material. It is useful as a rating device when selecting appropriate lesson material.

An Instrument for the Assessment of Instructional Materials

		Yes	No
I.	Objectives		
A.	Are there objectives stated for the use of the material?	___	___
	1. General objectives?	___	___
	2. Instructional objectives?	___	___
	3. Are the objectives stated in behavioral terms?	___	___
	4. If stated in behavioral terms, do the objectives specify:		
	a. the type of behavior?	___	___
	b. conditions under which it will appear?	___	___
	c. level of performance expected?	___	___
	5. List examples of objectives:		
B.	If there are no objectives stated for the use of the material, are the objectives instead implicit* or readily obvious?	___	___
	If yes, please outline below what objectives *you* believe govern the purpose of the material:		
C.	What appears to be the source of the objectives (both stated and implicit objectives)?		
	1. Are the objectives related to a larger frame of instruction?	___	___
	2. Are the objectives specific to a subject skill?	___	___
	3. Are the objectives related to a broader behavioral pattern that is to be developed over a period of time?	___	___

4. What seems to be the emphasis of the objectives? (Check as many as appropriate)

    a. Attitudinal   _____
    b. Motor skills   _____
    c. Cognitive development skills   _____
    d. Subject skills   _____

5. Are the objectives drawn from: (Check as many as appropriate)

    a. A learning approach?   _____
    b. Society needs? (Citizenship)   _____
    c. Demands of subject?   _____
    d. Demands and needs of child?   _____

D. Quantitative Rating of Objects

    (Directions: Please make an "x" on the rating scale below at the point which represents your best judgment on the following criteria. Please place the "x" *on* a specific point.)

1	2	3	4	5	6	7

Objectives vague, unclear, or missing. Those included not useful. Fail to distinguish between general and instructional objectives; mix various types of objectives, confusing to the teacher.

Average. Some of the criteria for objectives met, some missing; at times inconsistent. Objectives only partially operational for the classroom teacher.

Objectives stated clearly and in behavioral terms. Both general and instructional objectives stated in a consistent conceptual framework. Excellent, one of the best; useful for a teacher.

II. Organization of the Material (Scope and Sequence)

	Yes	No
A. Has a task analysis been made of the material and some relationship specified between the tasks?	_____	_____

B. If a task analysis has been made, what basis was used to organize the materials? (Check as many as appropriate)

	Yes	No
1. Errorless discrimination	_____	_____
2. Simple to complex	_____	_____
3. Figure-ground	_____	_____
4. General to specific	_____	_____
5. Logical order	_____	_____
6. Chronology	_____	_____

C. If no indication of a task analysis has been made, what assumptions do you believe the authors have made concerning the organization of the instructional sequence of the material?

	Yes	No
D. Is there a basis for the scope of the material included in the instructional package?	_____	_____

1. If there is a basis, is it related to:	Yes	No
a. a subject area?	_____	_____
b. a motor skill development?	_____	_____
c. a cognitive skill area?	_____	_____
d. an affective response system?	_____	_____
e. other (please specify) _____	_____	_____
2. Has the scope been subjected to analysis for:		
a. appropriateness to students?	_____	_____
b. relationship to other material?	_____	_____

	Yes	No

E. Is there a recommended sequence? _____ _____

    1. What is the basis of the recommended sequence? (Check as many as appropriate)

        a. interrelationships of a subject _____

        b. positive reinforcement and programmed sequence _____

        c. open-ended development of a generalization _____

        d. advanced organizer (cognitive) _____

        e. other (please specify) _____

        _____

F. Briefly outline the scope and sequence:

G. Quantitative Rating of Organization of the Materials (Scope and Sequence)

(Directions: Please make an "x" on the rating scale below at the point which represents your best judgment on the following criteria. Please place the "x" *on* a specific point.)

1	2	3	4	5	6	7

Sequence illogical or unstated; teacher is left to puzzle it out. Does not appear to have subjected material to any analysis to build an instructional design. Scope is uncertain, seems to contradict sequence. Little help unintentionally to teacher or children in organizing material.

Average in organization. Some help, but teacher must supply much of organizational sequence. Scope somewhat limited, may be too narrow (or broad). Sequence is not detailed enough, and may not have been tested with a range of children.

Excellent organization of scope and sequence. Conceptually developed, based on a consistent theory; task analysis or other appropriate investigation has been done. Tested for appropriateness of recommended sequence.

II. Methodology

	Yes	No

A. Does the author(s) and/or material suggest any methodological approach? _____ _____

B. Is the methodological approach, if suggested, specific to the mode of transaction? _____ _____

    1. Does the mode of transaction: (Check as many as appropriate)

        a. rely upon teacher-centric method (largely teacher directing)? _____ _____

        b. rely upon pupil-centric method (largely self-directing)? _____ _____

        c. require active participation by the students? _____ _____

        d. require passive participation by the students? _____ _____

        e. involve combination of active and passive participation by the students? _____ _____

        f. direct students' attention to method of learning as well as the learning product? _____ _____

        g. provide for variation among students, using several approaches to method? _____ _____

C. Does the methodology suggested require extensive   Yes   No
      preparation by the teacher?   _____   _____

     1.   How much deviation is permitted in method-
         ology?
         Much _____   Some _____   Little _____
     2.   Does the methodology require unusual skills
         obtained through specific training?   _____   _____
     3.   Is there any statement on how methodology
         was tested; any experimental evidence?   _____   _____
     4.   If you have tried the recommended methodol-
         ogy, how successful did it seem for your
         students?

         Most succeeded _____
         About half succeeded _____
         Few succeeded _____

       a.   Please provide a brief description of the
          students who *were* successful and those
          who *were not* successful.

       b.   What variations on recommended
          methodology have you used?

D. In a brief statement, describe the recommended
    methodology.

E. Quantitative Rating of Methodology

    (Directions: Please make an "x" on the rating scale below at the point which
    represents your best judgment on the following criteria. Please place the "x"
    on a specific point.)

1	2	3	4	5	6	7

Very little help given on methodology, or methodology too abstract and complex for most students and teachers. Methodology appears unrelated to content and an afterthought in the learning package. Too active or passive for most students. Teacher required to participate fully with too many students at every step. Does not have appropriate methodology for variety of learning ability among students.	Gives help to the teacher, but would like more. Some students would be able to cope with suggested methodology, but others not. Does not appear to have been widely field tested. Teacher has to work out variety for students with special learning difficulties.	Uses a variety of modes in the transactions. Does not chain a teacher to a mode without reason, but provides assistance for different abilities. Describes the field test of the methodology. Teachers will find methodology easy to use, and believe students will respond. Methodology part of goals of instruction and not just vehicle for content.

IV. Evaluation   Yes   No

    A.   Are there recommended evaluation procedures for
        teachers and students in the instructional package?   _____   _____

1. What do the evaluation procedures em-   Yes   No
    phasize? (Check as many as appropriate)

    a. Cognitive skills   _____
    b. Subject skills   _____
    c. Psychomotor skills   _____
    d. Affective responses   _____
2. Are the evaluation procedures compatible with
    the objectives?   _____   _____
3. Are evaluation procedures developed for
    several different levels? (Check as many as ap-
    propriate)

    a. immediate feedback evalua-
        tion for the pupil   _____
    b. evaluation for a variety of
        the areas in #1 above, and
        over a period of time   _____
    c. immediate feedback evalu-
        ation for the teacher   _____
    d. evaluation on a norm
        referent   _____
    e. evaluation on a criterion
        referent   _____

B. Are the evaluation procedures contained in the
    package?   _____   _____

C. Does the evaluation give attention to both product
    and process learning?   _____   _____

D. Is there information on how evaluation procedures
    were tested and developed?   _____   _____

E. Briefly state what evaluation procedures are includ-
    ed, if possible, and give examples:

F. Quantitative Rating of Evaluation

    (Directions: Please make an "x" on the rating scale below at the point which
    represents your best judgment on the following criteria. Place the "x" *on* a
    specific point.)

1	2	3	4	5	6	7

Haphazard in ap-
proach. Product and
process learnings either
entirely neglected or
confused. Lists items,
but poorly constructed;
no evidence of testing
of evaluation approach.
Students receive no as-
sistance through feed-
back. Fails to recognize
and examine different
types of learning where
appropriate.

Some examples given;
range of evaluation
limited. Samples given,
but limited and sketchy.
Teacher finds useful that
which is given, but
needs more examples.
Evaluation limited to
product or process. Un-
sure on whether evalua-
tion has ever been test-
ed, but seems logical
though limited in types
of learning examples.

Many suggestions and
helps in evaluation for
the teacher. Has crite-
rion-reference proce-
dures where appropri-
ate. Student obtains
assistance in learning
through feedback evalu-
ation. Gives attention to
several kinds of learn-
ing, consistent with ob-
jectives of learning
package.

From Maurice J. Eash, "Developing an Instrument for the Assessment of Instructional Materials
(Form IV)" (paper read at Annual Convention of the American Educational Research Association,
1970, Minneapolis), by permission.

GLOSSARY

Achievement test
A test that measures the extent to which a person has acquired specific knowledge of skills as the result of instruction.

Affect
A value, attitude, feeling, or predisposition that is intended to be acquired.

Affective domain
Those activities, tasks, and processes that involve "feeling" in the form of attending, responding, or valuing.

Aim
A philosophical goal.

Anecdotal record
An abbreviated factual description of a student's behaviors, customarily observed in relation to a particular event occurring in a school setting, which, along with other descriptions compiled over a period of time, provides a continued and integrated picture of behavioral changes.

Aptitude test
A standardized device yielding an indication of an individual's potentialities to succeed in certain future tasks, such as work in academic subjects.

Attitudes and values
Outcomes that reflect students' feelings and subjective reactions to themselves, others, and specific experiences. (Attitudes and values are usually measured by attitude scales.)

Attitude test
A scale designed to determine an individual's set or predisposition to react in a positive or negative manner toward a person, object, idea, happening, or institution.

Brainstorming
A technique of generating ideas among members of a group, characterized by fluency, flexibility, and originality.

Cognitive domain
Those activities, tasks, and processes that involve "thinking" in the form of knowing, understanding, applying, analyzing, synthesizing, or evaluating.

Concept
A group or category of events, objects, ideas, or people that shares one or more characteristics. A concept is usually labeled by a symbol, such as a word.

Conceptual map
A chart depicting the relationship among the important ideas identified for a course design.

Content
The basis by which learning activities and lessons are linked to each other, to goals, and to rationale.

Control group
A group that does *not* experience the instructional program to be evaluated and to whose outcomes the program or treatment group's outcomes are compared (also called the comparison group) in a summative evaluation.

Criterion-reference test
A device to ascertain an individual's status with respect to a defined set of criterion behaviors.

Curriculum
An organized set of objectives, lessons, and materials leading to the achievement of educational goals.

Educational goal
A desirable attribute of a person (e.g., literate, tolerant, creative) that is expected to result from the educational process.

Educational objective
A statement of desired or planned behavioral change.

Essay test
An examination in which the respondent is given an opportunity to write out his answers to each question in relatively great detail.

Evaluation

The process of judging the effectiveness—the strengths and weaknesses—of educational experiences in relation to certain goals and behaviorally stated objectives or criteria.

Formative evaluation

An examination of the outcomes of a group experiencing a program relative to the objectives of the program.

Goal

A general statement of the outcome of curriculum.

Group test

A test administered to several individuals simultaneously under relatively uniform (controlled) conditions involving standard directions and time limits.

Individual test

A test (e.g., certain intelligence scales and projective tests) administered to one person at a time.

Interest test

An instrument for assessing an individual's preferences, likes, or dislikes for certain activities, especially those connected with vocations or hobbies.

Matching test

An examination in which the examinee is required to pair each of several choices in one list of statements with an appropriate entry in a second list.

Mean

A measure of central tendency in which the sum of the scores of all individuals in a group is divided by the total frequency; the "average" score.

Measurement

The process of ordering individuals along a scale from high to low in terms of points they have earned on a test or been assigned by an observer.

Median

A measure of central tendency given by the point on the score scale that separates the upper 50 percent of the cases from the lower 50 percent; the "midpoint" score.

Mode

The score that occurs most often in a frequency distribution.

Multiple-choice test

An examination consisting of items beginning with a stem, premise, or lead statement for the completion of which the examinee is asked to choose the most nearly appropriate option from among several alternatives, the incorrect alternatives being called distractors.

Needs assessment
A public process where concerned parties contribute input to the curriculum process.

Norm
The typical performance of a reference group of examinees; a measure of standing devoid of qualitative judgment, such as the age level, grade level, or percentile rank of a given score relative to a standardization group.

Norm-referencing
Comparing individual test results to group results in order to report individual outcomes in terms of relative standing in the group (e.g., percent of test takers who got lower scores).

Objective test
An examination with an agreed-upon scoring key that allows for no differences in opinion concerning which item responses are to be scored right or wrong; a test permitting higher reliability in scoring than that usually afforded by the essay examination.

Performance test
A test that requires the examinee to use psychomotor responses, often involving manipulation of equipment, materials, or concrete objects.

Personality scale
A scale that furnishes measures of one or more dimensions of an individual's nonintellective or affective characteristics, in contrast to measures of cognitive characteristics, which test ability, achievement, or aptitude.

Psychomotor domain
Those activities and tasks that require sensorimotor functions and physical competencies, as distinguished from the cognitive or affective domains of behavior.

Random sample
A group of individuals chosen from a population in such a way that each member of the population had an equal probability of being selected; a sample permitting appropriate application of inferential statistical procedures of estimation and hypothesis testing.

Rationale
A statement justifying an educational experience in terms of its goals for the learner.

Raw score
The first score obtained on a test, such as the number of items correctly answered or the total number of points determined by simply summing credits assigned to two or more items.

Reliability
The extent to which a test is consistent over time and over items; that is,

whether it yields equivalent scores over testing occasions or over individual items or subparts of the test.

Sequence
The basis for ordering curriculum material in a particular manner.

Self-report inventory
A test or scale in which the examinee gives his responses to a number of questions concerned with his feelings or reactions to the information sought in the items.

Simple completion test
Typically an achievement examination in which the examinee fills in blanks that complete a stem or leading statement, the answer usually requiring from one to ten words.

Sociogram
A chart depicting the interpersonal relations of a group.

Summative evaluation
An examination of the outcomes of a group or groups experiencing the program to be evaluated in comparison to the outcomes of another similar group from which the program is withheld.

Systems approach
A planning tool organized to deal with a group of variables that affect each other; an experience-based model of a process to identify the elements, relationships, and sequences essential for a team of specialists to produce curriculum materials.

Taxonomy
A system of classification and the concepts underlying it.

Test
A more or less controlled task consisting of a group of questions or items that represent a sampling of behaviors to which points are assigned and totaled to yield a score.

Treatment group
Group that experiences the instructional program to be evaluated.

True-false test
An examination consisting of a series of statements the examinee identifies as correct or incorrect.

Validity
The extent to which a test measures what it is supposed to measure.

INDEX